The Big Ninja Foodi Pressure Cooker Cookbook

Easy & Delicious Recipes to Pressure Cook, Air Fry, Slow Cook, Dehydrate, and much more
(for Beginners and Advanced Users)

Kelly Brainerd

© Copyright 2020 - All rights reserved.

The content contained within this book may not be reproduced, duplicated or transmitted without direct written permission from the author or the publisher.

Under no circumstances will any blame or legal responsibility be held against the publisher, or author, for any damages, reparation, or monetary loss due to the information contained within this book. Either directly or indirectly.

Legal Notice:

This book is copyright protected. This book is only for personal use. You cannot amend, distribute, sell, use, quote or paraphrase any part, or the content within this book, without the consent of the author or publisher.

Disclaimer Notice:

Please note the information contained within this document is for educational and entertainment purposes only. All effort has been executed to present accurate, up to date, and reliable, complete information. No warranties of any kind are declared or implied. Readers acknowledge that the author is not engaging in the rendering of legal, financial, medical or professional advice. The content within this book has been derived from various sources. Please consult a licensed professional before attempting any techniques outlined in this book.

By reading this document, the reader agrees that under no circumstances is the author responsible for any losses, direct or indirect, which are incurred as a result of the use of information contained within this document, including, but not limited to, — errors, omissions, or inaccuracies.

Table of Contents

Introduction 5

Chapter 1: Breakfast Recipes 6

Egg in Toast 6
The Epic Fried Eggs 6
Gentle Keto Butter Fish 7
Tofu Scramble 7
Roasted Garlic Potatoes 8
Baked Eggs 8
Bacon & Scrambled Eggs 9
Avocado Egg 9
Breakfast Potatoes 10
Breakfast Frittata 10
Sensational Carrot Puree 11
Cheesy Broccoli Quiche 11
Omelette 12
Butter Melted Broccoli Florets 13
Eggs & Veggie Burrito 13
Egg & Turkey Sausage Cups 14
Breakfast Casserole 14

Chapter 2: Appetizers and Snack Recipes
.... 15

Seasoned Zucchini & Squash 15
Tarragon Yellow Squash 16
Cajun Spiced Zucchini 17
Basil Zucchini 17
Lemony Cauliflower 18
Feta Spinach 19
Seasoned Eggplant 20
Buttered Mashed Cauliflower 21
Glazed Carrots 22
Spicy Kale 22

Parmesan Mashed Cauliflower 23
Cauliflower with Capers 24

Chapter 3: Beef, Lamb and Pork Recipes
.... 26

Beef and Pork Chili Meal 26
Lamb Chops in Tomato Sauce 26
Lemon Pork Chops 27
Simple Strip Steak 28
Authentic Indian Beef Dish 28
Seasoned Filet Mignon 29
Lamb Meatballs in Mushroom Sauce 30
Original French Onion Pork Chops 31
Glazed Pork Ribs 32
Buttered Up Beef Meal 33
Excellent Mexican Beef Dish 33
Braised Leg of Lamb 34
Herbed Pork Chops 35
Effective New York Strip 36
Braised Rib-Eye Steak 37
Seasoned Pork Tenderloin 38
Braised Chuck Roast 39

Chapter 4: Chicken and Poultry Recipes 40

Parsley Duck Legs 40
Duck Pot Pie 41
Shredded Salsa Chicken 41
Spicy Whole Turkey 42
Mexican Chicken Soup 43
Hassel Back Chicken 44
Spinach Stuffed Chicken Breasts 44
Lemony Whole Chicken 46
Herbed Cornish Hen 47

Bacon-Wrapped Chicken Breasts 48
Garlic Chicken Thighs 49
Chicken with Veggies 50
Bruschetta Chicken Meal 51
Braised Turkey Breast 51
Duck Patties 52
Glazed Chicken Drumsticks 53
Turkey with Quinoa & Chickpeas 54

Chapter 5: Fish and Seafood Recipes 56

Garlic and Lemon Prawn Delight 56
Lovely Air Fried Scallops 56
Adventurous Sweet and Sour Fish 57
Packets of Lemon and Dill Cod 57
Awesome Cherry Tomato Mackerel 58
Lovely Carb Soup 59
The Rich Guy Lobster and Butter 59
Poached Chicken and Lime 60
Buttered Up Scallops 61
Fish & Chips with Herb Sauce 61
Southern Fried Fish Fillet 62
Fish Fillet with Pesto Sauce 63
Paprika Salmon 64
Fish Sticks 64
Awesome Sock-Eye Salmon 65
Ranch Fish Fillet 66
Fish & Fries 66

Chapter 6: Vegetarian Recipes 68

Tender Salsa 68
Parmesan Tomatoes 69
Mushroom and Pepper Quinoa 69
Turmeric Rice 70
Red Bean Stew 71

Zucchini Noodles 72
Refried Beans 72
Spicy Chinese Green Beans 73
Veggie Frittata 74
Mexican Style Quinoa 75
Quinoa health bowl 75
Bok Choy with Mustard Sauce 76
Romano Cheese Zucchini Circles 77
Spiced Veggie Lo Mein 78
Black Bean Chili 79
Pickled Garlic 80
Curried Chickpeas 81
Cloud Bread 82
Spiced Lentil Stew 83
Sweet Tomato Salsa 84
Asparagus Mash 85
Seasoned Eggs 86

Chapter 7: Dessert Recipes 87

Double Chocolate Cake 87
Chocolate Cheesecake 88
Lemon Cheesecake 89
Vanilla Cheesecake 90
Chocolate Walnut Cake 91
Chocolate Blackberry Cake 92
Strawberry Crumble 93
Mini Chocolate Cheesecakes 93
Raspberry Cobbler 94
Mini Vanilla Cheesecakes 95
Yogurt Cheesecake 96
Chocolate Brownie Cake 97
Lime Cheesecake 98
Mocha Cake 99

Introduction

The Ninja Foodi—The pressure cooker that crisps. Pressure cooker, air fryer, tender crisper. It comes with a 6.5-quart ceramic-coated pot with enough capacity to cook for your entire family. Whether you want to cook your meals faster or with less oil, Ninja Foodi has you covered. Tender crisp technology allows you to quickly cook ingredients, then the crisping lid gives your meals a crispy, golden finish.

The Ninja Foodi Pressure Cooker is very powerful. We need to understand its functions and store a variety of recipes so that we can maximize its value. So, we need professional books to guide the correct use.

The Big Ninja Foodi Pressure Cooker Cookbook will give you the perfect recipe. We tested the recipe extensively to ensure its quality. At the same time, we have accurate preparation time, cooking time, bill of materials, steps, and nutritional content data for each dish.

The book will provide you with a complete set of The Ninja Foodi Pressure Cooker Cookbook. The recipes include Breakfast, Beef and Pork, Chicken and Poultry, Fish and Seafood, Vegetarian Dishes, Dessert, etc. This book can fully meet your daily cooking needs.

Let the book help you enjoy the most beautiful food in the world.

Chapter 1: Breakfast Recipes

Egg in Toast

Prep Time: 15 minutes

Servings: 1

Ingredients:

- 1 slice bread
- 1 egg
- Salt and pepper to taste
- Cooking spray

Directions:

1. Spray a small baking pan with oil. Place the bread inside the pan.
2. Make a hole in the middle of the bread slice.
3. Crack open the egg and put it inside the hole.
4. Cover the Ninja Foodi with the crisping lid. Set it to air crisp.
5. Cook at 330 degrees for 6 minutes. Flip the toast and cook for 3 more minutes.

Serving Suggestion: Sprinkle with dried rosemary on top.

Tip: Aside from the salt and pepper, you can also season the egg with herbs like basil.

Nutrition:

Calories 92, Total Fat 5.2g, Saturated Fat 1.5g, Cholesterol 164mg, Sodium 123mg, Total Carbohydrate 5g, Dietary Fiber 0.3g, Total Sugars 0.7g, Protein 6.2g, Potassium 69mg

The Epic Fried Eggs

Prep time: 5 minutes

Cooking time: 10 minutes

Servings: 2

Ingredients

- 4 eggs
- 1/4 teaspoon ground black pepper
- 1 teaspoon butter, melted
- 3/4 teaspoon salt

Directions

Take a small egg pan and brush it with butter. Beat the eggs in the pan
Sprinkle with the ground black pepper and salt. Transfer the egg pan in the pot
Lower the Pressure Cooker lid. Cook the meat for 10 minutes at 350 F. Serve immediately and enjoy!

Nutrition:

Calories: 143, Fat: 10.2g, Carbohydrates: 0.9g, Protein: 11.4g

Gentle Keto Butter Fish

Prep time: 10 minutes

Cooking time: 30 minutes

Servings: 6

Ingredients

- 1 pound salmon fillets
- 2 tablespoons ginger/garlic paste
- 3 green chilies, chopped
- Salt and pepper to taste
- 3/4 cup butter

Directions

1. Season salmon fillets with ginger, garlic paste, salt, pepper
2. Place salmon fillets to Ninja Foodi and top with green chilies and butter
3. Lock lid and BAKE/ROAST for 30 minutes at 360 degrees F
4. Bake for 30 minutes and enjoy!

Nutrition:

Calories: 507, Fat: 45g, Carbohydrates: 3g, Protein: 22g

Tofu Scramble

Prep Time: 30 minutes

Servings: 4

Ingredients:

- 2 tablespoons olive oil, divided
- 2 tablespoons soy sauce
- 1/2 cup onion, chopped
- 1 teaspoon turmeric
- 1/2 teaspoon onion powder
- 1/2 teaspoon garlic powder
- 1 block firm tofu, sliced into cubes

Directions:

2. Mix all the ingredients except the tofu. Soak the tofu in the mixture.
3. Place the tofu in the Ninja Foodi pot. Seal the pot. Cover with the crisping lid.
4. Cook at 370 degrees F for 15 minutes.

Serving Suggestion: Garnish with scallions.

Tip: Press the tofu with paper towel to dry.

Nutrition:

Calories 90, Total Fat 8g, Saturated Fat 1.2g, Cholesterol 0mg, Sodium 455mg, Total Carbohydrate 3.2g, Dietary Fiber 0.7g, Total Sugars 1.1g, Protein 2.7g, Potassium 93mg

Roasted Garlic Potatoes

Prep Time: 30 minutes

Servings: 6

Ingredients:

- 2 lb. baby potatoes, sliced into wedges
- 2 tablespoons olive oil
- 2 teaspoons garlic salt

Directions:

1. Toss the potatoes in olive oil and garlic salt. Add the potatoes to the Ninja Foodi basket. Seal the crisping lid. Set it to air crisp. Cook at 390 degrees F for 20 minutes.

Serving Suggestion: Sprinkle dried herbs on top.

Tip: You can also use plain salt or garlic powder to season the potatoes.

Nutrition:

Calories 131, Total Fat 4.8g, Saturated Fat 0.7g, Cholesterol 0mg, Sodium 15mg, Total Carbohydrate 19.5g, Dietary Fiber 3.9g, Total Sugars 0.2g, Protein 4.1g, Potassium 635mg

Baked Eggs

Prep Time: 10 minutes

Servings: 1

Ingredients:

- Cooking spray
- 1 egg
- 1 tsp. dried rosemary
- Salt and pepper to taste

Directions:

1. Coat a ramekin with oil. Crack the egg into the ramekin.
2. Season with the rosemary, salt and pepper.
3. Close the crisping lid. Set it to air crisp. Cook at 330 degrees F for 5 minutes.

Serving Suggestion: Serve with toasted bread.

Tip: Try using other herbs to add flavor to the egg.

Nutrition:

Calories 72, Total Fat 5.1g, Saturated Fat 1.5g, Cholesterol 164mg, Sodium 62mg, Total Carbohydrate 1.2g, Dietary Fiber 0.5g, Total Sugars 0.3g, Protein 5.6g, Potassium 72mg

Bacon & Scrambled Eggs

Prep Time: 15 minutes

Servings: 2

Ingredients:

- 4 strips bacon
- 2 eggs
- 1 tablespoon milk
- Salt and pepper to taste

Directions:

1. Place the bacon inside the Ninja Foodi. Set it to air crisp.
2. Cover the crisping lid. Cook at 390 degrees for 3 minutes.
3. Flip the bacon and cook for another 2 minutes. Remove the bacon and set aside.
4. Whisk the eggs and milk in a bowl. Season with the salt and pepper.
5. Set the Ninja Foodi to sauté. Add the eggs and cook until firm.

Serving Suggestion: Serve with toasted bread.

Tip: You can add herbs to the egg.

Nutrition:

Calories 272, Total Fat 20.4g, Saturated Fat 6.7g, Cholesterol 206mg, Sodium 943mg, Total Carbohydrate 1.3g, Dietary Fiber 0g, Total Sugars 0.7g, Protein 19.9g, Potassium 279mg

Avocado Egg

Prep Time: 30 minutes

Servings: 2

Ingredients:

- 1 avocado, sliced in half and pitted
- 2 eggs
- Salt and pepper to taste
- 1/4 cup cheddar, shredded

Directions:

1. Crack the egg into the avocado slice. Season with the salt and pepper.
2. Put it on the Ninja Foodi basket. Seal the crisping lid.
3. Set it to air crisp. Cook at 400 degrees F for 15 minutes.
4. Sprinkle with the cheese 3 minutes before it is cooked.

Serving Suggestion: Garnish with fresh parsley.

Tip: You can also use mozzarella cheese for this recipe.

Nutrition:

Calories 281, Total Fat 23g, Saturated Fat 6g, Cholesterol 178mg, Sodium 158mg, Total Carbohydrates 9g, Dietary Fiber 6g, Protein 11g, Potassium 548mg

Breakfast Potatoes

Prep Time: 1 hour and 10 minutes
Servings: 2

Ingredients:

- 2 potatoes, scrubbed, rinsed and diced
- 1 tablespoon olive oil
- Salt to taste
- 1/4 teaspoon garlic powder

Directions:

1. Put the potatoes in a bowl of cold water. Soak for 45 minutes.
2. Pat the potatoes dry with paper towel. Toss in olive oil, salt and garlic powder.
3. Put in the Ninja Foodi basket. Seal the crisping lid. Set it to air crisp.
4. Cook at 400 degrees for 20 minutes. Flip the potatoes halfway through.

Serving Suggestion: Garnish with chopped parsley.
Tip: Cook the potatoes on a single layer. Do not overcrowd.

Nutrition:

Calories 208, Total Fat 7.2g, Saturated Fat 1.1g, Cholesterol 0mg, Sodium 90mg, Total Carbohydrate 33.7g, Dietary Fiber 5.1g, Total Sugars 2.5g, Protein 3.6g, Potassium 871mg

Breakfast Frittata

Prep Time: 35 minutes
Servings: 2

Ingredients:

- 1/4 lb. breakfast sausage, cooked and crumbled
- 4 eggs, beaten
- 1/2 cup cheddar cheese, shredded
- 1 red bell pepper, diced
- 1 green onion, chopped
- Cooking spray

Directions:

1. Mix the eggs, sausage, cheese, onion and bell pepper.
2. Spray a small baking pan with oil. Pour the egg mixture into the pan.
3. Set the basket inside the Ninja Foodi. Close the crisping lid.
4. Choose air crisp function. Cook at 360 degrees F for 20 minutes.

Serving Suggestion: Sprinkle chopped green onion on top.
Tip: You can also use yellow or green bell pepper to add color to the frittata.

Nutrition:

Calories 380, Total Fat 27.4g, Saturated Fat 12.0g, Cholesterol 443mg, Sodium 694mg, Total Carbohydrates 2.9g, Dietary Fiber 0.4g, Protein 31.2g, Sugars 1g, Potassium 328mg

Sensational Carrot Puree

Prep time: 10 minutes

Cooking time: 4 minutes |For 4 Servings:

Ingredients

- 1 and a 1/2 pound carrots, chopped
- 1 tablespoon of butter at room temperature
- 1 tablespoon of agave nectar
- 1/4 teaspoon of sea salt
- 1 cup of water

Directions

1. Clean and peel your carrots properly. Roughly chop up them into small pieces
2. Add 1 cup of water to your Pot
3. Place the carrots in a steamer basket and place the basket in the Ninja Foodi
4. Lock up the lid and cook on HIGH pressure for 4 minutes. Perform a quick release
5. Transfer the carrots to a deep bowl and use an immersion blender to blend the carrots
6. Add butter, nectar, salt, and puree. Taste the puree and season more if needed. Enjoy!

Nutrition:

Calories: 143, Fat: 9g, Carbohydrates: 16g, Protein: 2g

Cheesy Broccoli Quiche

Prep Time: 40 minutes

Servings: 2

Ingredients:

- 1 cup water
- 2 cups broccoli florets
- 1 carrot, chopped
- 1 cup cheddar cheese, grated
- 1/4 cup Feta cheese, crumbled
- 1/4 cup milk
- 2 eggs
- 1 teaspoon parsley
- 1 teaspoon thyme
- Salt and pepper to taste

Directions:

1. Pour the water inside the Ninja Foodi. Place the basket inside.
2. Put the carrots and broccoli on the basket. Cover the pot.

3. Set it to pressure. Cook at high pressure for 2 minutes.
4. Release the pressure quickly. Crack the eggs into a bowl and beat.
5. Season with the salt, pepper, parsley and thyme. Put the vegetables on a small baking pan. Layer with the cheese and pour in the beaten eggs Place on the basket.
6. Choose air crisp function. Seal the crisping lid. Cook at 350 degrees for 20 minutes.

Serving Suggestion: Garnish with chopped parsley or chives.

Tip: Try other types of cheese for this recipe.

Nutrition:

Calories 401, Total Fat 28g, Saturated Fat 16.5g, Cholesterol 242mg, Sodium 688mg, Total Carbohydrate 12.8g, Dietary Fiber 3.3g, Total Sugars 5.8g, Protein 26.2g, Potassium 537mg

Omelette

Prep Time: 15 minutes

Servings: 2

Ingredients:

- 2 eggs
- 1/4 cup milk
- 1 tablespoon red bell pepper, chopped
- 1 slice ham, diced
- 1 tablespoon mushrooms, chopped
- Salt to taste
- 1/4 cup cheese, shredded

Directions:

1. Whisk the eggs and milk in a bowl. Add the ham and vegetables. Season with the salt.
2. Pour the mixture into a small pan. Place the pan inside the Ninja Foodi basket.
3. Seal the crisping lid. Set it to air crisp. Cook at 350 degrees for 8 minutes.
4. Before it is fully cooked, sprinkle the cheese on top.
5. Coat the beef cubes with the salt and pickling spice.
6. In a skillet over medium heat, pour in the olive oil.

Nutrition:

Calories 177, Total Fat 11g, Saturated Fat 5.1g, Cholesterol 189mg, Sodium 425mg, Total Carbohydrate 7.1g, Dietary Fiber 1g, Total Sugars 4.8g, Protein 13.1g, Potassium 249mg

Butter Melted Broccoli Florets

Prep time: 10 minutes

Cooking time: 8 minutes

Servings: 4

Ingredients

- 4 tablespoons butter
- Salt and pepper to taste
- 2 pounds broccoli florets
- 1 cup whip cream

Directions

1. Arrange basket in the bottom of your Ninja Foodi and add water
2. Place florets on top of the basket. Lock lid and cook on HIGH pressure for 5 minutes
3. Quick release pressure and transfer florets to the pot itself
4. Season with salt, pepper and add butter
5. Lock crisping lid and Air Crisp on 360 degrees F 3 minutes
6. Transfer to a serving plate. Serve and enjoy!

Nutrition:

Calories: 178, Fat: 4g, Carbohydrates: 8g, Protein: 6g

Eggs & Veggie Burrito

Prep Time: 30 minutes

Servings: 8

Ingredients:

- 3 eggs, beaten
- Salt and pepper to taste
- Cooking spray
- 8 tortillas
- 2 red bell peppers, sliced into strips
- 1 onion, sliced thinly

Directions:

1. Beat the eggs in a bowl. Season with the salt and pepper. Set aside.
2. Choose sauté mode in the Ninja Foodi. Spray with the oil. Cook the vegetables until soft. Remove and set aside. Pour in the eggs to the pot. Cook until firm.
3. Wrap the eggs and veggies with tortilla.

Serving Suggestion: Sprinkle top part with cheese.

Tip: You can also add carrot sticks in this recipe.

Nutrition:

Calories 92, Total Fat 2.5g, Saturated Fat 0.6g, Cholesterol 61mg, Sodium 35mg, Total Carbohydrate 14.4g, Dietary Fiber 2.2g, Total Sugars 2.4g, Protein 3.9g, Potassium 143mg

Egg & Turkey Sausage Cups

Prep Time: 20 minutes

Servings: 4

Ingredients:

- 8 tablespoons turkey sausage, cooked and crumbled, divided
- 8 tablespoons frozen spinach, chopped and divided
- 8 teaspoons shredded cheddar cheese, divided
- 4 eggs

Directions:

1. Add a layer of the sausage, spinach and cheese on each muffin cup.
2. Crack the egg open on top. Seal the crisping lid. Set it to air crisp.
3. Cook at 330 degrees for 10 minutes.

Serving Suggestion: Sprinkle basil and Parmesan on top.

Tip: You can also use Monterey Jack cheese in place of cheddar.

Nutrition:

Calories 171, Total Fat 13.3g, Saturated Fat 4.7g, Cholesterol 190mg, Sodium 289mg, Total Carbohydrate 0.5g, Dietary Fiber 0.1g, Total Sugars 0.4g, Protein 11.9g, Potassium 161mg

Breakfast Casserole

Prep Time: 50 minutes

Servings: 4

Ingredients:

- Cooking spray
- 1 lb. hash browns
- 1 lb. breakfast sausage, cooked and crumbled
- 1 red bell pepper, diced
- 1 green bell pepper, diced
- 1 onion, diced
- 4 eggs
- Salt and pepper to taste

Directions:

1. Coat a small baking pan with oil. Place the hash browns on the bottom part.
2. Add the sausage, and then the onion and bell peppers.
3. Place the pan on top of the Ninja Foodi basket. Put the basket inside the pot.
4. Close the crisping lid. Set it to air crisp. Cook at 350 degrees F for 10 minutes.
5. Open the lid. Crack the eggs on top. Cook for another 10 minutes.
6. Season with the salt and pepper.

Nutrition:

Calories 513, Total Fat 34g, Saturated Fat 9.3g, Cholesterol 173mg, Sodium 867mg, Total Carbohydrate 30g, Dietary Fiber 3.1g, Total Sugars 3.1g, Protein 21.1g, Potassium 761mg

Chapter 2: Appetizers and Snack Recipes

Seasoned Zucchini & Squash

Prep Time: 15 minutes
Cooking time: 10 minutes
Servings: 6

Ingredients:

- 2 large yellow squash, cut into slices
- 2 large zucchinis, cut into slices
- ¼ cup olive oil
- ½ onion, sliced
- ¾ teaspoon Italian seasoning
- ½ teaspoon garlic salt
- ¼ teaspoon seasoned salt

Directions:

1. In a large bowl, mix together all the ingredients.
2. Arrange the greased "Cook & Crisp Basket" in the pot of Ninja Foodi.
3. Close the Ninja Foodi with crisping lid and select "Air Crisp".
4. Set the temperature to 400 degrees F for 5 minutes.
5. Press "Start/Stop" to begin preheating.
6. After preheating, open the lid.
7. Place the veggie mixture into the "Cook & Crisp Basket".
8. Close the Ninja Foodi with crisping lid and select "Air Crisp".
9. Set the temperature to 400 degrees F for 10 minutes.
10. Press "Start/Stop" to begin cooking.

Nutrition:

Calories: 113, Fats: 9g, Net Carbs: 4.4g, Carbs: 8g, Fiber: 3.6g, Sugar: 4g, Proteins: 2.8g, Sodium: 85mg

Tarragon Yellow Squash

Prep Time: 10 minutes

Cooking time: 15 minutes

Servings: 6

Ingredients:

- 4 teaspoons olive oil
- 2 pounds yellow squash, sliced
- 1 teaspoon kosher salt
- ½ teaspoon ground white pepper
- 1 tablespoon tarragon leaves, chopped

Directions:

1. In a large bowl, mix together the oil, yellow squash, salt and white pepper.
2. Arrange the greased "Cook & Crisp Basket" in the pot of Ninja Foodi.
3. Close the Ninja Foodi with crisping lid and select "Air Crisp".
4. Set the temperature to 400 degrees F for 5 minutes.
5. Press "Start/Stop" to begin preheating.
6. After preheating, open the lid.
7. Place the yellow squash into the "Cook & Crisp Basket".
8. Close the Ninja Foodi with crisping lid and select "Air Crisp".
9. Set the temperature to 400 degrees F for 15 minutes.
10. Press "Start/Stop" to begin cooking.
11. Toss the yellow squash 2-3 times.
12. Transfer the yellow squash into a bowl with tarragon leaves and mix till well.
13. Serve immediately.

Nutrition:

Calories: 52, Fats: 3.4g, Net Carbs: 3.6g, Carbs: 5.3g, Fiber: 1.7g, Sugar: 2.6g, Proteins: 1.9g, Sodium: 403mg

Cajun Spiced Zucchini

Prep Time: 10 minutes
Cooking time: 1 minute
Servings: 6

Ingredients:

- 4 zucchinis, sliced
- 1 tablespoon butter
- 2 tablespoons Cajun seasoning
- 1 teaspoon paprika
- 1 teaspoon garlic powder
- ½ cup water

Directions:

1. In the pot of Ninja Foodi, place all ingredients and stir to combine.
2. Close the Ninja Foodi with the pressure lid and place the pressure valve to "Seal" position.
3. Select "Pressure" and set to "Low" for 1 minute.
4. Press "Start/Stop" to begin cooking.
5. Switch the valve to "Vent" and do a "Quick" release.
6. Serve hot.

Nutrition:

Calories: 40, Fats: 2.2g, Net Carbs: 5g, Carbs: 8g, Fiber: 3g, Sugar: 4g, Proteins: 1.5g, Sodium: 78mg

Basil Zucchini

Prep Time: 10 minutes
Cooking time: 9 minutes
Servings: 5

Ingredients:

- 1 tablespoon olive oil
- 1 onion, chopped
- 1½ pounds zucchinis, chopped
- 2 garlic cloves, minced
- ½-¾ cup water
- Salt, as required
- 1 tablespoon fresh basil leaves, chopped

Directions:

1. Select "Sauté/Sear" setting of Ninja Foodi and place the oil into the pot.
2. Press "Start/Stop" to begin cooking and heat for about 2-3 minutes.
3. Add the onion and cook for about 4 minutes.
4. Press "Start/Stop" to stop cooking and stir in the zucchini, salt and water.
5. Close the Ninja Foodi with the pressure lid and place the pressure valve to "Seal" position.
6. Select "Pressure" and set to "High" for 3 minutes.
7. Press "Start/Stop" to begin cooking.
8. Switch the valve to "Vent" and do a "Natural" release.
9. Garnish with the basil and serve hot.

Nutrition:

Calories: 56, Fats: 3.1g, Net Carbs: 5g, Carbs: 7g, Fiber: 2g, Sugar: 3.3g, Proteins: 2g, Sodium: 46mg

Lemony Cauliflower

Prep Time: 15 minutes
Cooking time: 7 minutes
Servings: 8

Ingredients:

- 3 cauliflower heads, cut into florets
- 3 tablespoon fresh lemon juice
- 3 tablespoon olive oil
- Salt and ground black pepper, as required

Directions:

1. In the pot of Ninja Foodi, place 1 cup of water.
2. Arrange the "Reversible Rack "in the pot of Ninja Foodi.
3. Place the cauliflower florets pan over the "Reversible Rack".
4. Close the Ninja Foodi with the pressure lid and place the pressure valve to "Seal" position.
5. Select "Pressure" and set to "High" for 7 minutes.
6. Press "Start/Stop" to begin cooking.
7. Switch the valve to "Vent" and do a "Natural" release.

8. Transfer the cauliflower in a large serving bowl.
9. Add the oil lemon juice, salt and black pepper and toss to coat well.
10. Serve immediately.

Nutrition:

Calories: 71, Fats: 5.4g, Net Carbs: 2.9g, Carbs: 95.4g, Fiber: 2.5g, Sugar: 2g, Proteins: 1.5g, Sodium: 50mg

Feta Spinach

Prep Time: 10 minutes
Cooking time: 15 minutes
Servings: 6

Ingredients:

- 2 pounds fresh spinach, chopped
- 1 garlic clove, minced
- 1 jalapeño pepper, minced
- 4 tablespoons butter, melted
- Salt and ground black pepper, as required
- 1 cup feta cheese, crumbled
- 1 teaspoon fresh lemon zest, grated

Directions:

1. In a bowl, add the spinach, garlic, jalapeño, butter, salt and black pepper and mix well.
2. Arrange the "Cook & Crisp Basket" in the pot of Ninja Foodi.
3. Close the Ninja Foodi with crisping lid and select "Air Crisp".
4. Set the temperature to 340 degrees F for 5 minutes.
5. Press "Start/Stop" to begin preheating.
6. After preheating, open the lid.
7. Place the spinach mixture into the "Cook & Crisp Basket".
8. Close the Ninja Foodi with crisping lid and select "Air Crisp".
9. Set the temperature to 340 degrees F for 15 minutes.
10. Press "Start/Stop" to begin cooking.
11. Immediately, stir in the cheese and lemon zest and serve hot.

Nutrition:

Calories: 169, Fats: 13.6g, Net Carbs: 3.2g, Carbs: 6.6g, Fiber: 3.4g, Sugar: 1.7g, Proteins: 8g, Sodium: 480mg

Seasoned Eggplant

Prep Time: 10 minutes

Cooking time: 20 minutes

Servings: 4

Ingredients:

- 1 large eggplant, cut into 1-inch pieces
- 2 tablespoons olive oil
- 1 teaspoon garlic powder
- 1 teaspoon sweet paprika
- ½ teaspoon red pepper flakes
- ½ teaspoon Italian seasoning
- Salt, as required

Directions:

1. In a large bowl, mix together all the ingredients.
2. Arrange the greased "Cook & Crisp Basket" in the pot of Ninja Foodi.
3. Close the Ninja Foodi with crisping lid and select "Air Crisp".
4. Set the temperature to 375 degrees F for 5 minutes.
5. Press "Start/Stop" to begin preheating.
6. After preheating, open the lid.
7. Place the eggplant pieces into the "Cook & Crisp Basket".
8. Close the Ninja Foodi with crisping lid and select "Air Crisp".
9. Set the temperature to 375 degrees F for 20 minutes.
10. Press "Start/Stop" to begin cooking.
11. Shake the basket once halfway through.

Nutrition:

Calories: 99, Fats: 7.5g, Net Carbs: 4.2g, Carbs: 8.7g, Fiber: 4.5g, Sugar: 4g, Proteins: 1.5g, Sodium: 103mg

Buttered Mashed Cauliflower

Prep Time: 15 minutes

Cooking time: 10 minutes

Servings: 8

Ingredients:

- 4 tablespoons butter, divided
- ½ onion, chopped roughly
- 3 pounds cauliflower florets, chopped roughly
- 8-10 garlic cloves, chopped
- Salt, as required
- ½ cup homemade vegetable broth
- Ground black pepper, as required
- 3 tablespoons fresh chives, minced

Directions:

1. Select "Sauté/Sear" setting of Ninja Foodi and place 3 tablespoons of the butter into the pot.

2. Press "Start/Stop" to begin cooking and heat for about 2-3 minutes.

3. Add the onion and cook for about 2-3 minutes.

4. Add the cauliflower, carrots, parsnip, garlic and salt and cook for about 1-2 minutes.

5. Press "Start/Stop" to stop cooking and stir in the broth and black pepper.

6. Close the Ninja Foodi with the pressure lid and place the pressure valve to "Seal" position.

7. Select "Pressure" and set to "High" for 5 minutes.

8. Press "Start/Stop" to begin cooking.

9. Switch the valve to "Vent" and do a "Natural" release.

10. Add the remaining butter and with an immersion blender, blend until smooth.

11. Serve with the garnishing of chives.

Nutrition:

Calories: 103, Fats: 6.1g, Net Carbs: 5.5g, Carbs: 10g, Fiber: 4.5g, Sugar: 4.5g, Proteins: 4g, Sodium: 160mg

Glazed Carrots

Prep Time: 10 minutes
Cooking time: 4 minutes
Servings: 8

Ingredients:

- 1 (2-pound bag baby carrots
- ½ cup powdered Erythritol
- 4 tablespoons butter, chopped
- Salt, as required
- ½ cup homemade vegetable broth

Directions:

1. In the pot of Ninja Foodi, place all ingredients and stir to combine.
2. Close the Ninja Foodi with the pressure lid and place the pressure valve to "Seal" position.
3. Select "Pressure" and set to "High" for 4 minutes.
4. Press "Start/Stop" to begin cooking.
5. Switch the valve to "Vent" and do a "Quick" release.
6. Serve hot.

Nutrition:

Calories: 92, Fats: 5.9g, Net Carbs: 5g, Carbs: 8g, Fiber: 3g, Sugar: 4g, Proteins: 1.5g, Sodium: 182mg

Spicy Kale

Prep Time: 10 minutes
Cooking time: 3 minutes
Servings: 3

Ingredients:

- 2 tablespoons butter
- 1 teaspoon cumin seeds
- 2 garlic cloves, chopped finely
- 1 (10-ounce package fresh baby kale
- ½ teaspoon red chili powder
- ¼ teaspoon ground coriander
- ¼ teaspoon ground turmeric
- Salt, as required

- ¼ cup water

Directions:

1. Select "Sauté/Sear" setting of Ninja Foodi and place the butter into the pot.
2. Press "Start/Stop" to begin cooking and heat for about 2-3 minutes.
3. Add the cumin seeds and sauté for about 30 seconds.
4. Stir in the garlic and sauté for about 30 seconds.
5. Press "Start/Stop" to stop cooking and stir in the kale, spices and salt.
6. Close the Ninja Foodi with the pressure lid and place the pressure valve to "Seal" position.
7. Select "Pressure" and set to "Low" for 3 minutes.
8. Press "Start/Stop" to begin cooking.
9. Switch the valve to "Vent" and do a "Quick" release.
10. Select "Sauté/Sear" setting of Ninja Foodi and cook for about 2-3 minutes.
11. Press "Start/Stop" to stop cooking and serve hot.

Nutrition:

Calories: 109, Fats: 7.9g, Net Carbs: 5.5g, Carbs: 8g, Fiber: 2.5g, Sugar: 0.1g, Proteins: 3.7g, Sodium: 167mg

Parmesan Mashed Cauliflower

Prep Time: 15 minutes
Cooking time: 10 minutes
Servings: 4

Ingredients:

- 1 head cauliflower, leaves removed and stemmed
- 1 cup homemade vegetable broth
- 4 garlic cloves, chopped
- 6 fresh thyme sprigs
- ½ cup Parmesan cheese, grated
- ½ cup plain Greek yogurt
- Salt and ground black pepper, as required

Directions:

1. In the pot of Ninja Foodi, place the broth, garlic and thyme.
2. Arrange the "Reversible Rack" in the pot of Ninja Foodi.

3. Close the Ninja Foodi with the pressure lid and place the pressure valve to "Seal" position.

4. Select "Pressure" and set to "High" for 10 minutes.

5. Press "Start/Stop" to begin cooking.

6. Switch the valve to "Vent" and do a "Quick" release.

7. Transfer the cauliflower into a bowl with a little liquid from pot.

8. Add the cheese, yogurt, salt and black pepper and with an immersion blender, blend until smooth.

9. Serve immediately.

Nutrition:

Calories: 90, Fats: 3.2g, Net Carbs: 4.9g, Carbs: 7g, Fiber: 1.9g, Sugar: 4g, Proteins: 8.5g, Sodium: 358mg

Cauliflower with Capers

Prep Time: 15 minutes
Cooking time: 13 minutes
Servings: 4

Ingredients:

- 1 medium head cauliflower
- ½ cup water
- ¼ cup olive oil
- 4 garlic cloves, minced
- 2 tablespoons capers, minced
- 1 teaspoon red pepper flakes, crushed
- ½ cup Parmesan cheese, grated

Directions:

1. With a knife, cut an X into the cauliflower head, slicing about halfway down.

2. In the pot of Ninja Foodi, place ½ cup of water.

3. Place the cauliflower head into the "Cook & Crisp Basket".

4. Arrange the "Cook & Crisp Basket" in the pot.

5. Close the Ninja Foodi with the pressure lid and place the pressure valve to "Seal" position.

6. Select "Pressure" and set to "Low" for 3 minutes.

7. Press "Start/Stop" to begin cooking.

8. Switch the valve to "Vent" and do a "Quick" release.

9. Meanwhile, in a small bowl, add the oil, garlic, capers and red pepper flakes and mix well.

10. Place the oil mixture over the cauliflower evenly and sprinkle with the Parmesan cheese.

11. Now, close the Ninja Foodi with crisping lid and select "Air Crisp".

12. Set the temperature to 390 degrees F for 5 minutes.

13. Press "Start/Stop" to begin cooking.

14. Serve warm.

Nutrition:

Calories: 149, Fats: 14g, Net Carbs: 3g, Carbs: 5g, Fiber: 2g, Sugar: 1.7g, Proteins: 3.7g, Sodium: 192mg

Chapter 3: Beef, Lamb and Pork Recipes

Beef and Pork Chili Meal

Prep Time: 10 minutes

Cooking Time: 35 minutes

Servings: 4

Ingredients:

- 1 pound ground beef
- 1 pound ground pork
- 3 tomatillos, chopped
- 1 teaspoon garlic powder
- 1 jalapeno pepper
- 1 tablespoon ground cumin
- 1 tablespoon chili powder
- Salt as needed

Directions:

1. Set your Ninja Foodi to Saute mode and add beef and pork, brown them slightly
2. Add the rest of the ingredients to the pot onion, tomatillo, garlic, tomato paste, jalapeno, cumin, water, chili powder
3. Mix well
4. Lock up the lid and cook on HIGH Pressure for 35 minutes and release the Pressure naturally
5. Serve and enjoy!

Nutrition:

Calories: 325, Fat: 23 g, Saturated Fat: 5 g, Carbohydrates: 6 g, Fiber: 2 g, Sodium: 394 mg, Protein: 20 g

Lamb Chops in Tomato Sauce

Prep Time: 10 mins

Cooking Time: 10 hours

Number of Servings 4

Ingredients:

- 1 pound lamb chops
- 1½ cups tomatoes, chopped finely
- 1 cup chicken broth

- Salt and ground black pepper, as required
- 3 tablespoon mixed fresh herbs (oregano, thyme, sage), chopped

Directions:

1. In the pot of Ninja Foodi, place all the ingredients and mix well.
2. Close the Ninja Foodi with crisping lid and select "Slow Cooker".
3. Set on "Low" for 8 hours.
4. Press "Start/Stop" to begin cooking.
5. Open the lid and serve hot.

Nutrition:

Calories: 371, Fat: 19.1g, Saturated Fat: 6.2g, Trans Fat: 12.9g, Carbohydrates: 4.5g, Fiber 1.2g, Sodium 255mg, Protein: 45.4g

Lemon Pork Chops

Prep Time: 10 minutes
Cooking Time: 5 minutes
Servings: 4

Ingredients:

- ½ cup hot sauce
- ½ cup of water
- 2 tablespoons butter
- 1/3 cup lemon juice
- 1 pound pork cutlets
- **½ teaspoon paprika**

Directions:

1. Add listed ingredients to your Ninja Foodi cook and crisp basket, place the basket inside
2. Lock lid and cook on HIGH Pressure for 5 minutes, release Pressure naturally over 10 minutes
3. Gently stir and serve, enjoy!

Nutrition:

- Calories: 414, Fat: 21g, Saturated Fat: 4 g, Carbohydrates: 3 g, Fiber: 2 g, Sodium: 520 mg, Protein: 50 g

Simple Strip Steak

Prep Time: 10 mins

Cooking Time: 8 mins

Servings: 2

Ingredients:

- 1 (9½-ounce) New York strip steak
- Salt and ground black pepper, as required
- 1 teaspoon olive oil

Directions:

1. Coat the steak with oil and then generously season with salt and black pepper.
2. Arrange the greased "Cook & Crisp Basket" in the pot of Ninja Foodi.
3. Close the Ninja Foodi with crisping lid and select "Air Crisp".
4. Set the temperature to 400 degrees F for 5 minutes.
5. Press "Start/Stop" to begin preheating.
6. After preheating, open the lid.
7. Place the steak into the "Cook & Crisp Basket".
8. Close the Ninja Foodi with crisping lid and select "Air Crisp".
9. Set the temperature to 400 degrees F for 8 minutes.
10. Press "Start/Stop" to begin cooking.
11. Open the lid and place the steak onto a cutting board for about 10 minutes before slicing.
12. Cut into desired sized slices and serve.

Nutrition:

Calories: 186, Fat: 7g, Saturated Fat: 2.4g, Trans Fat: 4.6g, Carbohydrates: 0g, Fiber 0g, Sodium 177 mg, Protein: 30.2g

Authentic Indian Beef Dish

Prep Time: 10 minutes
Cooking Time: 20 minutes
Servings: 4

Ingredients:

- ½ yellow onion, chopped
- 1 tablespoon olive oil
- 2 garlic cloves, minced

- 1 jalapeno pepper, chopped
- 1 cup cherry tomatoes, quartered
- 1 teaspoon fresh lemon juice
- 1-2 pounds grass-fed ground beef
- 1-2 pounds fresh collard greens, trimmed and chopped

Spices

- 1 teaspoon cumin, ground
- ½ teaspoon ginger, ground
- 1 teaspoon coriander, ground
- ½ teaspoon fennel seeds, ground
- ½ teaspoon cinnamon, ground
- Salt and pepper to taste
- ½ teaspoon turmeric, ground

Directions:

1. Set your Ninja Foodi to Saute mode, add garlic and onion, Saute for 3 minutes
2. Add Jalapeno pepper, beef, spices and stir
3. Lock lid and cook on MEDIUM pressure for 15 minutes
4. Release pressure naturally
5. Add tomatoes,s collard, Saute for 3 minutes
6. Stir in lemon juice, salt, and pepper
7. Stir gently
8. Transfer dish to a serving bowl
9. Serve and enjoy!

Nutrition:

Calories: 409, Fat: 16g, Saturated Fat: 4 g, Carbohydrates: 5 g, Fiber: 1 g, Sodium: 744 mg, Protein: 56 g

Seasoned Filet Mignon

Prep Time: 10 mins

Cooking Time: 7 mins

Servings: 4

Ingredients:

- 4 (8-ounce) filet mignon
- ¼ cup avocado oil
- 2 tablespoons steak seasoning
- 1 tablespoon salt

Directions:

1. Coat both sides of each filet mignon with oil and then rub with steak seasoning and salt.
2. Arrange the "Reversible Rack" in the pot of Ninja Foodi.
3. Close the Ninja Foodi with crisping lid and select "Broil" for 5 minutes.
4. Press "Start/Stop" to begin preheating.
5. After preheating, open the lid.
6. Place the filets mignon over the "Reversible Rack".
7. Close the Ninja Foodi with crisping lid and select "Broil" for 8 minutes.
8. Press "Start/Stop" to begin cooking.
9. Open the lid and place the filets onto a platter for about 5 minutes before serving.

Nutrition:

Calories: 425, Fat: 16.7g, Saturated Fat: 6.1g, Trans Fat: 10.1g, Carbohydrates: 0.8g, Fiber 0.6g, Sodium 1878mg, Protein: 63.9g

Lamb Meatballs in Mushroom Sauce

Prep Time: 15 mins

Cooking Time: 22 mins

Servings: 6

Ingredients:

- 1½ pounds ground lamb
- 2 tablespoons dried onion, minced
- ¼ cup fresh parsley, minced
- 2 teaspoons dried sage
- ½ teaspoon fennel seeds, crushed
- ½ teaspoon ground nutmeg
- ½ teaspoon garlic powder
- Salt and ground black pepper, as required
- 8 ounces fresh button mushrooms, sliced
- 1 large onion, chopped
- ¼ cup beef broth
- ¼ cup low-sodium soy sauce
- 2 tablespoons cornstarch
- ½ cup unsweetened coconut milk

Directions:

1. In a large bowl, add the lamb, dried onion, parsley, sage, fennel seeds, nutmeg, garlic powder, salt and black pepper and mix until well combined.
2. Make 1-inch meatballs from the mixture.
3. In the pot of Ninja Foodi, place the mushrooms, onion, broth and soy sauce and stir to combine.
4. Arrange the meatballs on top of the mushroom mixture.
5. Close the Ninja Foodi with the pressure lid and place the pressure valve to "Seal" position.

6. Select "Pressure" and set to "High" for 20 minutes.
7. Press "Start/Stop" to begin cooking.
8. Switch the valve to "Vent" and do a "Quick" release.
9. Meanwhile, in a small bowl, add the cornstarch and coconut milk and mix well.
10. Open the lid and select "Sauté/Sear" setting of Ninja Foodi.
11. Stir in the cornstarch mixture cook for about 1-2 minutes.
12. Press "Start/Stop" to stop cooking and serve hot.

Nutrition:

Calories: 285, Fat: 13.4g, Saturated Fat: 7.3g, Trans Fat: 6.1g, Carbohydrates: 6.5g, Fiber 1.2g, Sodium 739mg, Protein: 34.6g

Original French Onion Pork Chops

Prep Time: 10 minutes
Cooking Time: 9 minutes
Servings: 4

Ingredients:

- 4 pork chops
- 10 ounces French Onion Soup
- ½ cup sour cream
- 10 ounces chicken broth

Directions:

1. Add pork chops to your Ninja Foodi
2. Add broth
3. Lock lid and cook on HIGH Pressure for 12 minutes
4. Release Pressure naturally over 10 minutes
5. Whisk sour cream and French Onion Soup and pour mixture over pork
6. Set your Ninja Foodi to Saute mode and cook for 6-8 minutes more
7. Serve and enjoy!

Nutrition:

Calories: 356, Fat: 26g, Saturated Fat: 10 g, Carbohydrates: 7g, Fiber: 2 g, Sodium: 648 mg, Protein: 21g

Glazed Pork Ribs

Prep Time: 15 mins

Cooking Time: 30 mins

Servings: 6

Ingredients:

- 2 pounds pork baby back ribs
- 2 bay leaves
- 4 garlic cloves, minced
- 2 tablespoons mixed dried herbs
- Salt and ground black pepper, as required
- 4 cups water
- ½ cup BBQ sauce

Directions:

1. In the pot of Ninja Foodi, add all ingredients except BBQ sauce and stir to combine.
2. Close the Ninja Foodi with the pressure lid and place the pressure valve to "Seal" position.
3. Select "Pressure" and set to "High" for 20 minutes.
4. Press "Start/Stop" to begin cooking.
5. Do a "Natural" release.
6. Open the lid and transfer the pork ribs onto a cutting board for about 5 minutes.
7. With paper towels, pat dry the ribs completely.
8. Transfer the ribs into a baking pan with BBQ sauce and mix well.
9. Cover and refrigerate for about 2-3 hours.
10. Arrange the "Reversible Rack" in the pot of Ninja Foodi.
11. Close the Ninja Foodi with crisping lid and select "Broil" for 5 minutes.
12. Press "Start/Stop" to begin preheating.
13. After preheating, open the lid.
14. Place the baking pan of pork ribs over the "Reversible Rack".
15. Close the Ninja Foodi with crisping lid and select "Broil" for 10 minutes.
16. Press "Start/Stop" to begin cooking.
17. Flip the ribs once halfway through.
18. Open the lid and serve immediately.

Nutrition:

Calories: 586, Fat: 45.1g, Saturated Fat: 18.2g, Trans Fat: 26.9g, Carbohydrates: 8.2g, Fiber 0.2g, Sodium 362mg, Protein: 34.4g

Buttered Up Beef Meal

Prep Time: 10 minutes
Cooking Time: 60 minutes
Servings: 4

Ingredients:

- 3 pounds beef roast
- 1 tablespoon olive oil
- 2 tablespoons Keto-Friendly ranch dressing
- 1 jar pepper rings, with juices
- 8 tablespoons butter
- 1 cup of water

Directions:

1. Set your Ninja Foodi to Saute mode and add 1 tablespoon of oil
2. Once the oil is hot, add roast and sear both sides
3. Set the Saute off and add water, seasoning mix, reserved juice, and pepper rings on top of your beef
4. Lock up the lid and cook on HIGH Pressure for 60 minutes
5. Release the Pressure naturally over 10 minutes
6. Cut the beef with salad sheers and serve with pureed cauliflower
7. Enjoy!

Nutrition:

Calories: 365, Fat: 18g, Saturated Fat: 5 g, Carbohydrates: 12g, Fiber: 3 g, Sodium: 1558 mg, Protein: 16 g

Excellent Mexican Beef Dish

Prep Time: 10 minutes
Cooking Time: 12 minutes
Servings: 4

Ingredients:

- 2 and ½ pounds boneless beef short ribs
- 1 tablespoon chili powder
- 1 and ½ teaspoons salt
- 1 tablespoon fat
- 1 medium onion, thinly sliced
- 1 tablespoon tomato sauce
- 6 garlic cloves, peeled and smashed

- ½ cup roasted tomato salsa
- ½ cup bone broth
- Fresh ground black pepper
- ½ cup cilantro, minced
- 2 radishes, sliced

Directions:

1. Take a large-sized bowl and add salt, beef, chili powder. Gently stir
2. Set your Ninja Foodi to Saute mode, add butter and let it melt
3. Add garlic, tomato paste, Saute for 30 seconds
4. Add beef stock, fish sauce
5. Lock lid and cook on HIGH Pressure for 35 minutes (MEAT/STEW Mode)
6. Naturally release Pressure, seasoning according to your taste
7. Enjoy!

Nutrition:

Calories: 308, Fat: 18g, Saturated Fat: 2 g, Carbohydrates: 21 g, Fiber: 2 g, Sodium: 1014 mg, Protein: 38 g

Braised Leg of Lamb

Cooking Time: 75 mins

Servings: 6

Ingredients:

- 1 (4-pound) bone-in leg of lamb
- Salt and ground black pepper, as required
- 1 tablespoon olive oil
- 1 large yellow onion, sliced thinly
- 1½ cups chicken broth, divided
- 2 tablespoons fresh lemon juice
- 6 garlic cloves, crushed
- 6 fresh thyme sprigs
- 3 fresh rosemary sprigs

Directions:

1. Season the leg of lamb with salt and black pepper generously
2. Select "Sauté/Sear" setting of Ninja Foodi and place the butter into the pot.
3. Press "Start/Stop" to begin cooking and heat for about 2-3 minutes.
4. Add the leg of lamb and sear for about 4 minutes per side.
5. Transfer the leg of the lamb onto a large plate.

6. In the pot, add the onion and a little salt and cook for about 3 minutes.
7. Add a little broth and cook for about 2 minutes, scraping the brown bits from the bottom.
8. Press "Start/Stop" to stop cooking and stir in the cooked leg of lamb and remaining ingredients.
9. Close the Ninja Foodi with the pressure lid and place the pressure valve to "Seal" position.
10. Select "Pressure" and set to "High" for 75 minutes.
11. Press "Start/Stop" to begin cooking.
12. Do a "Natural" release.
13. Open the lid and with tongs, transfer the leg of lamb onto a cutting board for about 10 minutes.
14. Strain the pan liquid into a bowl.
15. Cut the leg of lamb into desired sized slices.
16. Pour strained liquid over the sliced leg of lamb and serve.

Nutrition:

Calories: 626, Fat: 42.3g, Saturated Fat: 19.5g, Trans Fat: 22.8g, Carbohydrates: 2.6g, Fiber 0.6g, Sodium 303mg, Protein: 54.4g

Herbed Pork Chops

Prep Time: 15 mins

Cooking Time: 12 mins

Servings: 2

Ingredients:

- 2 garlic cloves, minced
- ½ tablespoon fresh cilantro, chopped
- ½ tablespoon fresh rosemary, chopped
- ½ tablespoon fresh parsley, chopped
- 2 tablespoons olive oil
- ¾ tablespoon Dijon mustard
- 1 tablespoon ground coriander
- 1 teaspoon sugar
- Salt, as required
- 2 (6-ounces) (1-inch thick) pork chops

Directions:

1. In a bowl, mix together the garlic, herbs, oil, mustard, coriander, sugar, and salt.
2. Add the pork chops and generously coat with marinade.
3. Cover and refrigerate for about 2-3 hours.
4. Remove the chops from the refrigerator and set aside at room temperature for about 30 minutes.

5. Arrange the greased "Cook & Crisp Basket" in the pot of Ninja Foodi.
6. Close the Ninja Foodi with crisping lid and select "Air Crisp".
7. Set the temperature to 390 degrees F for 5 minutes.
8. Press "Start/Stop" to begin preheating.
9. After preheating, open the lid.
10. Place the chops into the "Cook & Crisp Basket".
11. Close the Ninja Foodi with crisping lid and select "Air Crisp".
12. Set the temperature to 390 degrees F for 12 minutes.
13. Press "Start/Stop" to begin cooking.
14. Open the lid and serve hot.

Nutrition:

Calories: 683, Fat: 56.7g, Saturated Fat: 17.9g, Trans Fat: 38.8g, Carbohydrates: 3.9g, Fiber 0.6g, Sodium 265mg, Protein: 38.8g

Effective New York Strip

Prep Time: 10 minutes
Cooking Time: 9 minutes
Servings: 4

Ingredients:

- 24 ounces NY strip steak
- ½ teaspoon ground black pepper
- 1 teaspoon salt

Directions:

1. Add steaks on a metal trivet, place it on your Ninja Foodi
2. Season with salt and pepper
3. Add 1 cup water to the pot
4. Close the lid
5. Cook for 1 minute on HIGH
6. Quick-release Pressure
7. Place Air-crisp lid and Air Crisp for 8 minutes for a medium-steak
8. Serve and enjoy!

Nutrition:

Calories: 503, Fat: 46g, Saturated Fat: 12 g, Carbohydrates: 1g, Fiber: 0 g, Sodium: 898 mg, Protein: 46g

Braised Rib-Eye Steak

Prep Time: 10 mins

Cooking Time: 16 mins

Servings: 6

Ingredients:

- 1 (2-pound) rib-eye steak
- 2 tablespoons steak rub
- 2 tablespoons butter
- 2 cups beef broth

Directions:

1. Season the steak with steak rub evenly and set aside for about 10 minutes.
2. Select "Sauté/Sear" setting of Ninja Foodi and place the butter into the pot.
3. Press "Start/Stop" to begin cooking and heat for about 2-3 minutes.
4. Add the steak and cook, uncovered for about 3 minutes per side.
5. Press "Start/Stop" to stop cooking and stir in the broth.
6. Close the Ninja Foodi with pressure lid and place the pressure valve to "Seal" position.
7. Select "Pressure" and set to "High" for 10 minutes.
8. Press "Start/Stop" to begin cooking.
9. Switch the valve to "Vent" and do a "Quick" release.
10. Open the lid and place the steak onto a cutting board for about 5 minutes before slicing.
11. Cut the steak into desired-sized slices and serve.

Nutrition:

Calories: 469, Fat: 37.8g, Saturated Fat: 15.9g, Trans Fat: 21.9g, Carbohydrates: 1.3g, Fiber 0g, Sodium 589mg, Protein: 28.4g

Seasoned Pork Tenderloin

Prep Time: 10 mins

Cooking Time: 30 mins

Servings: 6

Ingredients:

- 2 pounds pork loin
- 2 tablespoons olive oil, divided
- 2-3 tablespoons barbecue seasoning rub

Directions:

1. Arrange a wire rack in a baking pan.
2. Coat the pork loin with oil evenly and then rub with barbecue seasoning rub generously.
3. Arrange the pork loin into the prepared baking pan.
4. Arrange the "Reversible Rack" in the pot of Ninja Foodi.
5. Close the Ninja Foodi with crisping lid and select "Bake/Roast".
6. Set the temperature to 350 degrees F for 5 minutes.
7. Press "Start/Stop" to begin preheating.
8. After preheating, open the lid.
9. Place the pan over the "Reversible Rack".
10. Close the Ninja Foodi with crisping lid and select "Bake/Roast".
11. Set the temperature to 350 degrees F for 30 minutes.
12. Press "Start/Stop" to begin cooking.
13. Open the lid and place the pork loin onto a cutting board.
14. With a piece of foil, cover the pork loin for about 10 minutes before slicing.
15. With a sharp knife, cut the pork loin into desired sized slices and serve.

Nutrition:

Calories: 421, Fat: 25.7g, Saturated Fat: 8.6g, Trans Fat: 17.1g, Carbohydrates: 2g, Fiber 0g, Sodium 304mg, Protein: 41.3g

Braised Chuck Roast

Prep Time: 10 mins

Cooking Time: 1 hour 16 minutes

Servings: 8

Ingredients:

- 2 tablespoons coconut oil
- 3 pounds chuck roast
- 1 medium onion, sliced
- 1 teaspoon salt
- 2 cups water

Directions:

1. Select "Sauté/Sear" setting of Ninja Foodi and place the oil into the pot.
2. Press "Start/Stop" to begin cooking and heat for about 2-3 minutes.
3. Add the roast and cook for about 2-3 minutes per side.
4. Press "Start/Stop" to stop cooking and sprinkle the roast with salt.
5. Top with onion, followed by the water.
6. Close the Ninja Foodi with the pressure lid and place the pressure valve to "Seal" position.
7. Select "Pressure" and set to "High" for 70 minutes.
8. Press "Start/Stop" to begin cooking.
9. Do a "Natural" release.
10. Open the lid and place the roast onto a cutting board for about 10-15 minutes before slicing.
11. Cut into desired-sized slices and serve.

Nutrition:

Calories: 402, Fat: 17.5g, Saturated Fat: 8.1g, Trans Fat: 9.4g, Carbohydrates: 1.3g, Fiber 0.3g, Sodium 404mg, Protein: 56.3g

Chapter 4: Chicken and Poultry Recipes

Parsley Duck Legs

Prep Time: 10 mins

Cooking Time: 30 mins

Servings: 2

Ingredients:

- 2 garlic cloves, minced
- 1 tablespoon fresh parsley, chopped
- 1 teaspoon five-spice powder
- Salt and ground black pepper, as required
- 2 duck legs

Directions:

1. In a bowl, mix together garlic, parsley, five-spice powder, salt and black pepper.
2. Rub the duck legs with garlic mixture generously.
3. Arrange the "Cook & Crisp Basket" in the pot of Ninja Foodi.
4. Close the Ninja Foodi with crisping lid and select "Air Crisp".
5. Set the temperature to 340 degrees F for 5 minutes.
6. Press "Start/Stop" to begin preheating.
7. After preheating, open the lid.
8. Place the duck legs into the "Cook & Crisp Basket".
9. Close the Ninja Foodi with crisping lid and select "Air Crisp".
10. Set the temperature to 340 degrees F for 25 minutes.
11. Press "Start/Stop" to begin cooking.
12. After 25 minutes of cooking, set the temperature to 390 degrees F for 5 minutes.
13. Open the lid and serve hot.

Nutrition:

Calories: 434, Fat: 14.4g, Saturated Fat: 3.2g, Trans Fat: 11.2g, Carbohydrates: 1.1g, Fiber: 0.1g, Sodium: 339mg, Protein: 70.4g

Duck Pot Pie

Prep Time: 10 minutes
Cooking time: 50 minutes
Servings: 8

Ingredients:
- 7 ounces keto dough
- 1 teaspoon onion powder
- 1 pound duck breast
- ½ teaspoon anise
- 1 cup green beans
- 1 cup cream
- 1 egg
- 1 teaspoon salt

Directions:
1. Place the duck breast on the trivet and transfer the trivet into the pressure cooker. Set the pressure cooker to "Steam" mode. Steam the duck for 25 minutes. When the cooking time ends, remove the duck from the pressure cooker and shred it well. Place the shredded duck in the mixing bowl. Add onion powder, anise, cream, salt, and green beans and stir well. Beat the egg. Roll the keto dough and cut it into two parts. Put the one part of the bread dough into the pressure cooker and make the pie crust. Transfer filling in the pie crust and cover it with the second part of the dough. Spread the pie with the whisked egg and close the lid. Cook the dish on "Pressure" mode for 25 minutes. When the cooking time ends, let the pot pie rest briefly. Transfer it to a serving plate, cut it into slices and serve.

Nutrition:
calories 194, fat 5.6, fiber 3.8, carbs 7.8, protein 28

Shredded Salsa Chicken

Prep Time: 5 minutes
Cooking Time: 20 minutes
Servings: 4

Ingredients:
- 1 pound chicken breast, skin and bones removed
- 1 cup chunky salsa Keto friendly
- ½ teaspoon salt
- Pinch of oregano
- ¾ teaspoon cumin
- Pepper to taste

Directions:
1. Season chicken with all the listed spices, then add to Ninja Foodi
2. Cover with salsa and close the lid
3. Cook on HIGH pressure for 20 minutes
4. Quick-release the pressure
5. Add chicken to a platter then shred the chicken
6. Serve and enjoy!

Nutrition:
Calories: 125, Fat: 3g, Carbohydrates: 2g, Protein: 22g, Sodium: 703mg, Fiber: 1g, Saturated Fat: 1g

Spicy Whole Turkey

Prep Time: 15 mins

Cooking Time: 8 hours 5 minutes

Servings: 14

Ingredients:

For Spice Rub:
- 2 teaspoons dried thyme, crushed
- 2 teaspoons ground cumin
- 2 teaspoons paprika
- 2 teaspoons salt
- 1 teaspoon ground white pepper
- 1 teaspoon ground black pepper

For Turkey:
- 1 (8-pound) whole turkey, necks, and giblets removed
- 4 garlic cloves, peeled and smashed
- ½ of medium onion, chopped
- 2 carrots, scrubbed and cut into thirds
- 2 celery stalks, cut into thirds
- 1 whole lemon, quartered

Directions:
1. For the spice rub: in a bowl, mix all ingredients. Keep aside.
2. Rinse turkey well, and with a paper towel, pat dries completely.
3. Fold back the wings of the turkey.
4. Rub smashed garlic over outside of turkey evenly.
5. Rub inside and outside of turkey with spice rub generously.

6. Place lemon quarters in the cavity of the turkey.
7. Tie the legs of the turkey with kitchen twine.
8. In the pot of a Ninja Foodi, place the onion, carrots, celery, and 3 garlic cloves.
9. Arrange turkey over vegetables.
10. Close the Ninja Foodi with crisping lid and select "Slow Cooker".
11. Set on "High" for 6-8 hours.
12. Press "Start/Stop" to begin cooking.
13. Now, close the Ninja Foodi with crisping lid and select "Broil" for 5 minutes.
14. Press "Start/Stop" to begin cooking.
15. Open the lid and place the turkey onto a platter for about 25-30 minutes before slicing.
16. Cut into desired sized pieces and serve alongside vegetables.

Nutrition:

Calories: 403, Fat: 18.6g, Saturated Fat: 5.8g, Trans Fat: 12.8g, Carbohydrates: 2.2g, Fiber 0.6g, Sodium 1175mg, Protein: 48.9g

Mexican Chicken Soup

Prep Time: 5 minutes
Cooking Time: 20 minutes
Servings: 4

Ingredients:
- 2 cups chicken, shredded
- 1/3 cup salsa
- 4 tablespoons olive oil
- 1 teaspoon garlic powder
- ½ cup scallions, chopped
- 4 ounces green chilies, chopped
- 1 cup celery root, chopped
- 1 teaspoon cumin
- ½ teaspoon habanero, minced
- ½ cup cilantro, chopped
- 8 cups chicken broth
- 1 teaspoon onion powder
- Salt and pepper to taste

Directions:
1. Add all the listed ingredients to your Ninja Foodi
2. Stir and close the lid

3. Cook on HIGH pressure for 10 minutes
4. Release the pressure naturally over 10 minutes
5. Serve and enjoy!

Nutrition:

Calories: 204, Fat: 14g, Carbohydrates: 4g, Protein: 14g, Sodium: 31mg, Fiber: 2g, Saturated Fat: 2g

Hassel Back Chicken

Prep Time: 5 minutes

Cooking Time: 1 hour

Servings: 4

Ingredients:
- 8 large chicken breasts
- 2 cups fresh mozzarella cheese, thinly sliced
- 4 large Roma tomatoes, thinly sliced
- 4 tablespoons butter
- Salt and pepper to taste

Directions:
1. Add chicken breasts, season with salt and pepper to make deep slits
2. Stuff with mozzarella cheese slices and tomatoes in your chicken slits
3. Grease Ninja Foodi pot with butter
4. Arrange stuffed chicken breasts
5. Close the lid and BAKE/ROAST for 1 hour at 365 degrees F
6. Serve and enjoy!

Nutrition:

Calories: 278, Fat: 15g, Carbohydrates: 3.8g, Protein: 15g, Sodium: 441mg, Fiber:1g, Saturated Fat 3g:

Spinach Stuffed Chicken Breasts

Prep Time: 15 mins

Cooking Time: 30 mins

Servings: 2

Ingredients:
- 1 tablespoon olive oil
- 1¾ ounces fresh spinach
- ¼ cup ricotta cheese, shredded
- 2 (4-ounce) skinless, boneless chicken breasts

- Salt and ground black pepper, as required
- 2 tablespoons cheddar cheese, grated
- ¼ teaspoon paprika

Directions:

1. Select the "Sauté/Sear" setting of Ninja Foodi and place the oil into the pot.
2. Press "Start/Stop" to begin cooking and heat for about 2-3 minutes.
3. Add the spinach and cook for about 3-4 minutes.
4. Stir in the ricotta and cook for about 40-60 seconds.
5. Press "Start/Stop" to stop cooking and transfer the spinach mixture into a bowl.
6. Set aside to cool.
7. Cut slits into the chicken breasts about ¼-inch apart but not all the way through.
8. Stuff each chicken breast with the spinach mixture.
9. Sprinkle each chicken breast with salt and black pepper and then with cheddar cheese and paprika.
10. Arrange the greased "Cook & Crisp Basket" in the pot of Ninja Foodi.
11. Close the Ninja Foodi with a crisping lid and select "Air Crisp."
12. Set the temperature to 390 degrees F for 5 minutes.
13. Press "Start/Stop" to begin preheating.
14. After preheating, open the lid.
15. Place the chicken breasts into the "Cook & Crisp Basket."
16. Close the Ninja Foodi with a crisping lid and select "Air Crisp."
17. Set the temperature to 390 degrees F for 25 minutes.
18. Press "Start/Stop" to begin cooking.
19. Open the lid and serve hot.

Nutrition:

Calories: 279, Fat: 16 g, Saturated Fat: 5.6 g, Trans Fat: 10.4 g, Carbohydrates: 2.7 g, Fiber 0.7 g, Sodium 220 mg, Protein: 31.4 g

Lemony Whole Chicken

Prep Time: 15 mins

Cooking Time: 1 hour 29 minutes

Servings: 10

Ingredients:

- 1 (6-pound) whole chicken, necks and giblets removed
- Salt and ground black pepper, as required
- 3 fresh rosemary sprigs, divided
- 1 lemon, zested and cut into quarters
- 2 large onions, sliced,
- 4 cups chicken broth

Directions:

1. Stuff the cavity of chicken with 2 rosemary sprigs and lemon quarters.
2. Season the chicken with salt and black pepper evenly.
3. Chop the remaining rosemary sprig and set aside.
4. Select "Sauté/Sear" setting of Ninja Foodi and place the chicken into the pot.
5. Press "Start/Stop" to begin and cook, uncovered for about 5-7 minutes per side.
6. Remove chicken from the pot and place onto a roasting rack.
7. In the pot, place the onions and broth.
8. Arrange the "Reversible Rack" over the broth mixture.
9. Arrange the roasting rack on top of "Reversible Rack".
10. Sprinkle the chicken with reserved chopped rosemary and lemon zest.
11. Close the Ninja Foodi with crisping lid and select "Bake/Roast".
12. Set the temperature to 375 degrees F for 1¼ hours.
13. Press "Start/Stop" to begin cooking.
14. Open the lid and place the chicken onto a cutting board for about 10 minutes before carving.
15. Cut into desired sized pieces and serve.

Nutrition:

Calories: 545, Fat: 20.8g, Saturated Fat: 5.7g, Trans Fat: 15.1g, Carbohydrates: 3.3g, Sodium 556mg, Protein: 81g

Herbed Cornish Hen

Prep Time: 15 mins

Cooking Time: 16 mins

Servings: 6

Ingredients:

- ½ cup olive oil
- 1 teaspoon fresh rosemary, chopped
- 1 teaspoon fresh thyme, chopped
- 1 teaspoon fresh lemon zest, grated finely
- ¼ teaspoon sugar
- ¼ teaspoon red pepper flakes, crushed
- Salt and ground black pepper, as required
- 2 pounds Cornish game hen, backbone removed and halved

Directions:

1. In a large bowl, mix well all ingredients except hen portions.
2. Add the hen portions and coat with marinade generously.
3. Cover and refrigerator for about 2-24 hours.
4. In a strainer, place the hen portions to drain any liquid.
5. Arrange the greased "Cook & Crisp Basket" in the pot of Ninja Foodi.
6. Close the Ninja Foodi with crisping lid and select "Air Crisp".
7. Set the temperature to 390 degrees F for 5 minutes.
8. Press "Start/Stop" to begin preheating.
9. After preheating, open the lid.
10. Place the hen portions into the "Cook & Crisp Basket".
11. Close the Ninja Foodi with crisping lid and select "Air Crisp".
12. Set the temperature to 390 degrees F for 16 minutes.
13. Press "Start/Stop" to begin cooking.
14. Open the lid and place the hen portions onto a cutting board.
15. Cut each portion in 2 pieces and serve hot.

Nutrition:

Calories: 681, Fat: 57.4g, Saturated Fat: 12.7g, Trans Fat: 44.7g, Carbohydrates: 0.8g, Fiber 0.3g, Sodium 180mg, Protein: 38.2g

Bacon-Wrapped Chicken Breasts

Prep Time: 20 mins

Cooking Time: 20 mins

Servings: 4

Ingredients:

- 1 tablespoon sugar
- 8 fresh basil leaves
- 2 tablespoons red boat fish sauce
- 2 tablespoons water
- 2 (8-ounce) boneless chicken breasts, cut each breast in half horizontally
- Salt and ground black pepper, as required
- 8 bacon strips
- 1 tablespoon honey

Directions:

1. In a small heavy-bottomed pan, add the sugar over medium-low heat and cook for about 2-3 minutes or caramelized, stirring continuously.
2. Stir in the basil, fish sauce, and water.
3. Remove from heat and transfer into a large bowl.
4. Sprinkle the chicken with salt and black pepper.
5. Add the chicken pieces in the basil mixture and coat generously.
6. Refrigerate to marinate for about 4-6 hours.
7. Wrap each chicken piece with 2 bacon strips.
8. Coat each chicken piece with honey slightly.
9. Arrange the greased "Cook & Crisp Basket" in the pot of Ninja Foodi.
10. Close the Ninja Foodi with a crisping lid and select "Air Crisp."
11. Set the temperature to 365 degrees F for 5 minutes.
12. Press "Start/Stop" to begin preheating.
13. After preheating, open the lid.
14. Place the chicken breasts into the "Cook & Crisp Basket."
15. Close the Ninja Foodi with a crisping lid and select "Air Crisp."
16. Set the temperature to 365 degrees F for 20 minutes.
17. Press "Start/Stop" to begin cooking.
18. Open the lid and serve hot.

Nutrition:

Calories: 564, Fat: 32.6g, Saturated Fat: 10.3g, Trans Fat: 22.3g, Carbohydrates: 8.2g, Fiber 0g, Sodium 2100mg, Protein: 56.3g

Garlic Chicken Thighs

Prep Time: 15 minutes
Cooking time: 40 minutes
Servings: 6

Ingredients:
- 1 tablespoon garlic powder
- ⅓ cup garlic
- ½ lemon
- 1 teaspoon onion powder
- 2 tablespoons mayonnaise
- 1 teaspoon ground white pepper
- 1 tablespoon butter
- 1 teaspoon cayenne pepper
- pound 1 pound chicken thighs
- 4 ounces celery root

Directions:
1. Peel the garlic cloves and mince them. Combine the garlic with the chicken thighs and using a combine using your hands.
2. Sprinkle the meat with the onion powder, ground white pepper, cayenne pepper, and butter. Peel the celery root and grate it.
3. Chop the lemon into thin slices. Add the celery root and lemon in the chicken mixture.
4. Add garlic powder and mayonnaise, stir well and transfer it to the pressure cooker.
5. Set the pressure cooker to" Sear/Sauté" mode. Close the lid and cook the dish on poultry mode for 40 minutes.
6. When the cooking time ends, open the pressure cooker lid and transfer the cooked chicken into serving bowls.

Nutrition:

calories 142, fat 5.7, fiber 1, carbs 5.7, protein 17

Chicken with Veggies

Prep Time: 20 mins

Cooking Time: 8 hours 40 minutes

Servings: 8

Ingredients:

- 2 pounds skinless, boneless chicken breast tenders
- 1 large onion, chopped
- 2 cups asparagus, trimmed and cut into 2-inch pieces
- 1 tablespoon fresh thyme, chopped
- 1 teaspoon garlic powder
- Salt and ground black pepper, as required
- 4 medium zucchinis, spiralized with blade C
- 1 cup sour cream
- 1 cup cheddar cheese, shredded

Directions:

1. In the pot of Ninja Foodi, add the chicken, onion, asparagus, thyme, garlic powder, salt, and black pepper and mix well.
2. Close the Ninja Foodi with a crisping lid and select "Slow Cooker."
3. Set on "Low" for 8 hours.
4. Press "Start/Stop" to begin cooking.
5. Open the lid and
6. Place the zucchini noodles over the chicken mixture and top with cheese and cream.
7. Close the Ninja Foodi with a crisping lid and select "Slow Cooker."
8. Set on "Low" for 30-40 minutes.
9. Press "Start/Stop" to begin cooking.
10. Open the lid and stir the mixture well.
11. Serve hot.

Nutrition:

Calories: 292, Fat: 15g, Saturated Fat: 8.3g, Trans Fat: 6.7g, Carbohydrates: 8.2g, Fiber 2.3g Sodium 174mg, Protein: 32g

Bruschetta Chicken Meal

Prep Time: 5 minutes

Cooking Time: 9 minutes

Servings: 4

Ingredients:
- 2 pounds chicken breasts, quartered, boneless
- ½ cup sun-dried tomatoes, in olive oil
- 2 tablespoons balsamic vinegar
- 1/3 cup olive oil
- 2 tablespoons fresh basil, chopped
- 2 teaspoons garlic cloves, minced
- ½ teaspoon salt
- 1 teaspoon black pepper

Directions:
1. Whisk in vinegar, oil, garlic, pepper, salt into a bowl
2. Fold in the tomatoes, basil and then add breast
3. Mix them well
4. Transfer to fridge, sit it for 30 minutes
5. Add everything to your Ninja Foodi and close the lid
6. Cook on High Pressure for 9 minutes
7. Quick-release the pressure
8. Serve and enjoy!

Nutrition:

Calories: 480, Fat: 26g, Carbohydrates: 4g, Protein: 52g, Sodium: 229mg, Fiber: 2g, Saturated Fat: 8g

Braised Turkey Breast

Prep Time: 15 mins

Cooking Time: 30 mins

Servings: 8

Ingredients:
- 1 celery stalk, chopped
- 1 large onion, chopped
- 1 tablespoon fresh thyme, minced
- 1 tablespoon fresh rosemary, minced
- 14 ounces chicken broth

- 1 (6½-pound) skin-on, bone-in turkey breast
- Salt and ground black pepper, as required
- 3 tablespoons cornstarch
- 3 tablespoons water

Directions:

1. In the pot of Ninja Foodi, place celery, onion, herbs, and broth.
2. Arrange turkey breast on top and sprinkle with salt and black pepper.
3. Close the Ninja Foodi with the pressure lid and place the pressure valve to "Seal" position.
4. Select "Pressure" and set to "High" for 30 minutes.
5. Press "Start/Stop" to begin cooking.
6. Switch the valve to "Vent" and do a "Quick" release.
7. Open the lid and transfer the turkey breast onto a cutting board.
8. With a slotted spoon, skim off the fat from the surface of broth. Then strain it, discarding solids.
9. In a small bowl, dissolve the cornstarch in water.
10. Return the broth in pot and select "Sauté/Sear" setting of Ninja Foodi.
11. Press "Start/Stop" to begin cooking.
12. Add the cornstarch mixture, stirring continuously and cook for about 3-4 minutes.
13. Press "Start/Stop" to stop cooking and transfer the gravy into a serving bowl.
14. Cut the turkey breast into desired sized slices and serve alongside the gravy.

Nutrition:

Calories: 655, Fat: 26.7g, Saturated Fat: 6.7g, Trans Fat:0 g, Carbohydrates: 5.2g, Fiber 0.8g, Sodium 641mg, Protein: 80.3g

Duck Patties

Prep Time: 10 minutes
Cooking time: 15 minutes
Servings: 6

Ingredients:

- 1 tablespoon mustard
- 1 teaspoon ground black pepper
- 9 ounces ground duck
- ½ cup parsley
- 1 teaspoon salt
- 1 tablespoon olive oil

- 1 teaspoon oregano
- 1 teaspoon red pepper
- ½ teaspoon cayenne pepper
- 1 tablespoon flax meal

Directions:

1. Combine the mustard, ground black pepper, ground duck, salt, oregano, red pepper, cayenne pepper, and flax meal together in a mixing bowl and stir well.
2. Wash the parsley and chop it.
3. Sprinkle the duck mixture with the chopped parsley and stir well.
4. Make medium-sized patties from the duck mixture.
5. Set the pressure cooker to" Sauté" mode. Pour the olive oil into the pressure cooker. Add the duck patties and cook the dish on sauté mode for 15 minutes or until browned on both sides. Serve immediately.

Nutrition:

calories 106, fat 6.9, fiber 1.3 carbs 3.3, protein 8.6

Glazed Chicken Drumsticks

Prep Time: 15 mins

Cooking Time: 25 mins

Servings: 4

Ingredients:

- ¼ cup Dijon mustard
- 1 tablespoon honey
- 2 tablespoons olive oil
- Salt and ground black pepper, as required
- 4 (6 ounces) chicken drumsticks

Directions:

1. In a bowl, add all the ingredients except the drumsticks and mix until well combined.
2. Add the drumsticks and coat with the mixture generously.
3. Refrigerate, covered to marinate overnight.
4. In the pot of Ninja Foodi, place 1 cup of water.
5. Arrange the greased "Cook & Crisp Basket" in the pot of Ninja Foodi.
6. Place the chicken drumsticks into the "Cook & Crisp Basket."
7. Close the Ninja Foodi with the pressure lid and place the pressure valve to the "Seal" position.
8. Select "Pressure" and set it to "High" for 6 minutes.

9. Press "Start/Stop" to begin cooking.
10. Switch the valve to "Vent" and do a "Quick" release.
11. Now, close the Ninja Foodi with a crisping lid and Select "Air Crisp."
12. Set the temperature to 320 degrees F for 12 minutes.
13. Press "Start/Stop" to begin cooking.
14. After 12 minutes of cooking, set the temperature to 355 degrees F for 5 minutes.
15. Open the lid and serve hot.

Nutrition:

Calories: 374, Fat: 17.3g, Saturated Fat: 3.6g, Trans Fat: 13.6g, Carbohydrates: 5.2g, Fiber 0.5g, Sodium 352mg, Protein: 47.5g

Turkey with Quinoa & Chickpeas

Prep Time: 15 mins

Cooking Time: 20 mins

Servings: 4

Ingredients:

- 1½ tablespoons olive oil
- 6 ounces skinless, boneless turkey breast, cubed
- 1 medium onion, chopped
- 1 small sweet potato, peeled and chopped
- 2 garlic cloves, minced
- 1 tablespoon red chili powder
- ¼ teaspoon red pepper flakes, crushed
- ¼ teaspoon ground cumin
- ¼ teaspoon ground coriander
- Salt, to taste
- 1 cup canned chickpeas, rinsed and drained
- ¼ cup uncooked quinoa
- 1 cup tomatoes, chopped finely
- 1½ cups chicken broth
- 1 tablespoon fresh lemon juice
- 2 tablespoons fresh cilantro, chopped

Directions:

1. Select "Sauté/Sear" setting of Ninja Foodi and place the oil into the pot.
2. Press "Start/Stop" to begin cooking and heat for about 2-3 minutes.

3. Add the turkey and cook for about 5 minutes or until browned completely.
4. With a slotted spoon, transfer the turkey into a bowl.
5. In the pot, add the onion and cook for about 5 minutes.
6. Add the sweet potato and cook for about 5 minutes.
7. Add the garlic and spices and cook for about 1 minute.
8. Press "Start/Stop" to stop cooking and stir in the turkey, chickpeas, quinoa, tomato and broth.
9. Close the Ninja Foodi with the pressure lid and place the pressure valve to "Seal" position.
10. Select "Pressure" and set to "High for 4 minutes.
11. Press "Start/Stop" to begin cooking.
12. Do a "Natural" release for about 10 minutes and then switch the valve to "Vent" to do a "Quick" release.
13. Open the lid and stir in the lemon juice and cilantro.
14. Serve hot.

Nutrition:

Calories: 390, Fat: 11.5g, Saturated Fat: 1.9g, Trans Fat: 9.6g, Carbohydrates: 49.8g, Fiber 12.3g, Sodium 387mg, Protein: 24.2g

Chapter 5: Fish and Seafood Recipes

Garlic and Lemon Prawn Delight

Prep time: 5 minutes

Cooking time: 5 minutes

Servings: 4

Ingredients:

- 2 tablespoons olive oil
- 1 pound prawns
- 2 tablespoons garlic, minced
- 2/3 cup fish stock
- 1 tablespoon butter
- 2 tablespoons lemon juice
- 1 tablespoon lemon zest
- Salt and pepper to taste

Directions:

1. Set your Ninja Foodi to Saute mode and add butter and oil, let it heat up
2. Stir in remaining ingredients. Lock lid and cook on LOW pressure for 5 minutes
3. Quick release pressure. Serve and enjoy!

Nutrition:

Calories: 236, Fat: 12g, Carbohydrates: 2g, Protein: 27g

Lovely Air Fried Scallops

Prep time: 5 minutes

Cooking time: 5 minutes

Servings: 4

Ingredients:

- 12 scallops
- 3 tablespoons olive oil
- Salt and pepper to taste

Directions:

1. Gently rub scallops with salt, pepper, and oil
2. Transfer to your Ninja Foodie's insert, and place the insert in your Foodi
3. Lock Air Crisping lid and cook for 4 minutes at 390 degrees F

4. Half through, make sure to give them a nice flip and keep cooking. Serve warm and enjoy!

Nutrition:

Calories: 372, Fat: 11g, Carbohydrates: 0.9g, Protein: 63g

Adventurous Sweet and Sour Fish

Prep time: 10 minutes
Cooking time: 6 minutes
Servings: 4

Ingredients:

- 2 drops liquid stevia
- 1/4 cup butter
- 1 pound fish chunks
- 1 tablespoon vinegar
- Salt and pepper to taste

Directions:

1. Set your Ninja Foodi to Saute mode and add butter, let it melt
2. Add fish chunks and Saute for 3 minutes. Add stevia, salt, and pepper, stir
3. Lock Crisping Lid and cook on "Air Crisp" mode for 3 minutes at 360 degrees F
4. Serve once done and enjoy!

Nutrition:

Calories: 274, Fat: 15g, Carbohydrates: 2g, Protein: 33g

Packets of Lemon and Dill Cod

Prep time: 10 minutes
Cooking time: 5-10 minutes
Servings: 4

Ingredients:

- 2 tilapia cod fillets
- Salt, pepper and garlic powder to taste
- 2 sprigs fresh dill
- 4 slices lemon
- 2 tablespoons butter

Directions:

1. Layout 2 large squares of parchment paper

2. Place fillet in center of each parchment square and season with salt, pepper and garlic powder
3. On each fillet, place 1 sprig of dill, 2 lemon slices, 1 tablespoon butter
4. Place trivet at the bottom of your Ninja Foodi. Add 1 cup water into the pot
5. Close parchment paper around fillets and fold to make a nice seal
6. Place both packets in your pot . Lock lid and cook on HIGH pressure for 5 minutes
7. Quick release pressure . Serve and enjoy!

Nutrition:

Calories: 259, Fat: 11g, Carbohydrates: 8g, Protein: 20g

Awesome Cherry Tomato Mackerel

Prep time: 5 minutes
Cooking time: 7 minutes
Servings: 4

Ingredients:

- 4 Mackerel fillets
- 1/4 teaspoon onion powder
- 1/4 teaspoon lemon powder
- 1/4 teaspoon garlic powder
- 1/2 teaspoon salt
- 2 cups cherry tomatoes
- 3 tablespoons melted butter
- 1 and 1/2 cups of water
- 1 tablespoon black olives

Directions:

1. Grease baking dish and arrange cherry tomatoes at the bottom of the dish
2. Top with fillets sprinkle all spices. Drizzle melted butter over
3. Add water to your Ninja Foodi
4. Lower rack in Ninja Foodi and place baking dish on top of the rack
5. Lock lid and cook on LOW pressure for 7 minutes. Quick release pressure. Serve and enjoy!

Nutrition:

Calories: 325, Fat: 24g, Carbohydrates: 2g, Protein: 21g

Lovely Carb Soup

Prep time: 5 minutes
Cooking time: 6-7 hours
Servings: 4

Ingredients:

- 1 cup crab meat, cubed
- 1 tablespoon garlic, minced
- Salt as needed
- Red chili flakes as needed
- 3 cups vegetable broth
- 1 teaspoon salt

Directions:

1. Coat the crab cubes in lime juice and let them sit for a while
2. Add the all ingredients (including marinated crab meat) to your Ninja Foodi and lock lid
3. Cook on SLOW COOK MODE (MEDIUM) for 3 hours
4. Let it sit for a while
5. Unlock lid and set to Saute mode, simmer the soup for 5 minutes more on LOW
6. Stir and check to season. Enjoy!

Nutrition:

Calories: 201, Fat: 11g, Carbohydrates: 12g, Protein: 13g

The Rich Guy Lobster and Butter

Prep time: 15 minutes
Cooking time: 20 minutes
Servings: 4

Ingredients:

- 6 Lobster Tails
- 4 garlic cloves,
- 1/4 cup butter

Directions:

1. Preheat the Ninja Foodi to 400 degrees F at first
2. Open the lobster tails gently by using kitchen scissors
3. Remove the lobster meat gently from the shells but keep it inside the shells
4. Take a plate and place it
5. Add some butter in a pan and allow it melt

6. Put some garlic cloves in it and heat it over medium-low heat
7. Pour the garlic butter mixture all over the lobster tail meat
8. Let the fryer to broil the lobster at 130 degrees F
9. Remove the lobster meat from Ninja Foodi and set aside
10. Use a fork to pull out the lobster meat from the shells entirely
11. Pour some garlic butter over it if needed. Serve and enjoy!

Nutrition:

Calories: 160, Fat: 1g, Carbohydrates: 1g, Protein: 20g

Poached Chicken and Lime

Prep Time: 5 minutes
Cooking Time: 10 minutes
Servings: 4

Ingredients:

- 3 pieces of 1/3 pounds each chicken breasts, meat
- 1 cup of coconut milk
- 1 cup chicken stock
- 1-ounce shallot, minced
- 1 ounces ginger, sliced
- 2 medium banana peppers
- 2 tablespoons fish sauce
- Juice of 1 lime, and zest

Directions:

1. Add all the listed ingredients to your Ninja Foodi
2. Stir and close the lid
3. Cook on HIGH pressure for 10 minutes
4. Quick release the pressure
5. Top with fresh cilantro
6. Serve and enjoy!

Nutrition:

Calories: 425, Fat: 33g, Carbohydrates: 9g, Protein: 24g, Sodium: 561mg, Fiber: 3g, Saturated Fat: 7g

Buttered Up Scallops

Prep time: 10 minutes
Cooking time: 5 minutes
Servings: 4

Ingredients:

- 4 garlic cloves, minced
- 4 tablespoons rosemary, chopped
- 2 pounds sea scallops
- 12 cup butter
- Salt and pepper to taste

Directions:

1. Set your Ninja Foodi to Saute mode and add butter, rosemary, and garlic
2. Saute for 1 minute. Add scallops, salt, and pepper
3. Saute for 2 minutes. Lock Crisping lid and Crisp for 3 minutes at 350 degrees F. Serve and enjoy!

Nutrition:

Calories: 279, Fat: 16g, Carbohydrates: 5g, Protein: 25g

Fish & Chips with Herb Sauce

Prep Time: 50 minutes
Servings: 4

Ingredients:

- 2 potatoes, sliced into strips
- Salt to taste
- 1/4 cup flour
- 1 egg
- 1 teaspoon Dijon mustard
- 3/4 cup seasoned panko bread crumbs
- 2 1/2 teaspoons olive oil
- 4 cod fish fillets

For the sauce:

- 1/4 cup light mayonnaise
- 2 tablespoons sour cream
- 2 tablespoons dill pickle, chopped
- 2 tablespoons red onion, chopped

- 1 tablespoon dill, chopped
- 1 tablespoon tarragon, chopped
- 2 teaspoons capers

Directions:

1. Soak the potato strips in a bowl of water for 30 minutes.
2. Drain the water and pat the potatoes dry using a paper towel.
3. Place the potato strips in the Ninja Foodi basket.
4. Seal the crisping lid and choose air crisp function.
5. Cook at 360 degrees for 25 minutes, turning once or twice.
6. Season with the salt. Put the flour in a bowl.
7. Beat the egg and add the mustard in another bowl.
8. Mix the oil and bread crumbs on a shallow plate.
9. Coat the fish with the flour then the egg mixture, and then the oil with crumbs. Place in the basket. Cook at 360 degrees for 10 minutes.
10. Mix all the ingredients for the sauce and serve with the fish and fries.

Serving Suggestion: Garnish with cucumber and tomato slices.

Tip: Add cayenne pepper to make the sauce spicy.

Nutrition:

Calories 409, Total Fat 12.1g, Saturated Fat 2.6g, Cholesterol 146mg, Sodium 426mg, Total Carbohydrate 27.9g, Dietary Fiber 3.2g, Total Sugars 2.6g, Protein 45.8g, Potassium 956mg

Southern Fried Fish Fillet

Prep Time: 30 minutes

Servings: 4

Ingredients:

- 2 lb. white fish fillet
- 1 cup low fat milk
- 1 lemon slice
- 1/2 cup mustard
- 1/2 cup cornmeal
- 1/4 cup all purpose flour
- 2 tablespoons dried parsley flakes
- Salt and pepper to taste
- 1/4 teaspoon chili powder
- 1/4 teaspoon garlic powder
- 1/4 teaspoon onion powder
- 1/4 teaspoon cayenne pepper

Directions:

1. Place the fish fillet in a bowl. Pour the milk over the fish fillet.
2. Squeeze lemon slice over the fish. Marinate for 15 minutes.
3. Spread the mustard on the fish fillets.
4. In another bowl, mix the rest of the ingredients.
5. Coat the fish fillets with the cornmeal mixture. Place on the Ninja Foodi basket.
6. Set it to air crisp. Seal the crisping lid. Cook at 390 degrees for 10 minutes.
7. Flip the fillets and cook for 5 more minutes.

Serving Suggestion: Serve with fresh green salad.

Tip: You can use Dijon mustard or yellow mustard for this recipe.

Nutrition:

Calories 595, Total Fat 24g, Saturated Fat 3.4g, Cholesterol 178mg, Sodium 184mg, Total Carbohydrate 28.4g, Dietary Fiber 4.5g, Total Sugars 4.8g, Protein 64.7g, Potassium 1221mg

Fish Fillet with Pesto Sauce

Prep Time: 20 minutes

Servings: 3

Ingredients:

- 3 white fish fillets
- 1 tablespoon olive oil
- Salt and pepper to taste
- 2 cups fresh basil leaves
- 2 cloves garlic, crushed
- 2 tablespoons pine nuts
- 1 tablespoon Parmesan cheese, grated
- 1 cup olive oil

Directions:

1. Coat the fish fillets with 1 tablespoon of olive oil. Season with the salt and pepper.
2. Place in the Ninja Foodi basket. Cook at 320 degrees for 8 minutes.
3. While waiting, mix the remaining ingredients in a food processor.
4. Pulse until smooth. Spread the pesto sauce on both sides of the fish before serving.

Serving Suggestion: Garnish with chopped pine nuts.

Tip: Pesto sauce can be prepared in advanced and chilled in the refrigerator for up to 3 days.

Nutrition:

Calories 383, Total Fat 22.6g, Saturated Fat 4.1g, Cholesterol 125mg, Sodium 188mg, Total Carbohydrate 2.2g, Dietary Fiber 0.5g, Total Sugars 0.3g, Protein 42.1g, Potassium 715mg

Paprika Salmon

Prep Time: 15 minutes

Servings: 2

Ingredients:

- 2 salmon fillets
- 2 teaspoons avocado oil
- 2 teaspoons paprika
- Salt and pepper to taste

Directions:

1. Coat the salmon with oil. Season with salt, pepper and paprika.
2. Place in the Ninja Foodi basket. Set it to air crisp function.
3. Seal the crisping lid. Cook at 390 degrees for 7 minutes.

Serving Suggestion: Garnish with lemon slices.

Tip: Cooking depends on the fish fillet thickness. You may need to cook longer for thicker cuts.

Nutrition:

Calories 248, Total Fat 11.9g, Cholesterol 78mg, Sodium 79mg, Total Carbohydrate 1.5g, Dietary Fiber 1g, Total Sugars 0.2g, Protein 34.9g, Potassium 748mg

Fish Sticks

Prep Time: 20 minutes

Servings: 2

Ingredients:

- 1 lb. cod, sliced into strips
- 1/2 cup tapioca starch
- 2 eggs
- 1 teaspoon dried dill
- Salt and pepper to taste
- 1 cup almond flour
- 1 teaspoon onion powder
- 1/2 teaspoon mustard powder
- 2 tablespoons avocado oil

Directions:

1. Pat the cod fillet strips dry using paper towel.
2. Place the tapioca starch in a bowl.
3. In another bowl, beat the eggs.

4. In a larger bowl, mix the dill, salt, pepper, almond flour, onion powder and mustard powder. Dip each strip in the first, second and third bowls.
5. Coat the Ninja Foodi basket with the avocado oil.
6. Place the fish strips inside. Cook at 390 degrees F for 5 minutes.

Serving Suggestion: Serve with tartar sauce.

Tip: You can also freeze the fish sticks and cook frozen. Just increase cooking time to 7 to 10 minutes.

Nutrition:

Calories 549, Total Fat 15g, Saturated Fat 2.6g, Cholesterol 288mg, Sodium 246mg, Total Carbohydrate 39.4g, Dietary Fiber 2.7g, Total Sugars 2.2g, Protein 61g, Potassium 695mg

Awesome Sock-Eye Salmon

Prep time: 5 minutes
Cooking time: 5 minutes
Servings: 4

Ingredients:

- 4 sockeye salmon fillets
- 1 teaspoon Dijon mustard
- 1/4 teaspoon garlic, minced
- 1/4 teaspoon onion powder
- 1/4 teaspoon lemon pepper
- 1/2 teaspoon garlic powder
- 1/4 teaspoon salt
- 2 tablespoons olive oil
- 1 and 1/2 cup of water

Directions:

1. Take a bowl and add mustard, lemon juice, onion powder, lemon pepper, garlic powder, salt, olive oil. Brush spice mix over salmon
2. Add water to Instant Pot. Place rack and place salmon fillets on rack
3. Lock lid and cook on LOW pressure for 7 minutes
4. Quick release pressure .Serve and enjoy!

Nutrition:

Calories: 353, Fat: 25g, Carbohydrates: 0.6g, Protein: 40g

Ranch Fish Fillet

Servings: 4

Prep Time: 20 minutes

Ingredients:

- 3/4 cup bread crumbs
- 1 packet dry ranch dressing mix
- 2 1/2 tablespoons vegetable oil
- 2 eggs, beaten
- 4 fish fillets

Directions:

1. Combine the bread crumbs and ranch mix in a bowl. Pour in the oil.
2. Dip each fish fillet into the egg and cover with the crumb mixture.
3. Place in the Ninja Foodi basket. Seal the lid. Select air crisp function.
4. Cook at 360 degrees F for 12 minutes, flipping halfway through.

Serving Suggestion: Garnish with lemon wedges.

Tip: For added flavor, season the fish with salt and pepper.

Nutrition:

Calories 425, Total Fat 25.4g, Saturated Fat 5.7g, Cholesterol 113mg, Sodium 697mg, Total Carbohydrate 30.4g, Dietary Fiber 1.4g, Total Sugars 1.4g, Protein 18.8g, Potassium 360mg

Fish & Fries

Prep Time: 30 minutes

Servings: 4

Ingredients:

- 1 lb. potatoes, sliced into strips
- 2 tablespoons olive oil
- Salt and pepper to taste
- 1/4 cup all purpose flour
- 1 egg
- 2 tablespoons water
- 2/3 cup cornflakes, crushed
- 1 tablespoon Parmesan cheese, grated
- 1 lb. cod fillets

Directions:

1. Coat the potato strips with oil, salt and pepper. Place in the Ninja Foodi basket.

2. Seal the crisping lid and set it to air crisp.
3. Cook at 400 degrees F for 10 minutes, stirring halfway through.
4. While waiting, combine the flour with salt and pepper in one bowl.
5. In another bowl, beat the egg and add water.
6. In the third bowl, mix the cornflakes and Parmesan.
7. Dip each fillet in the flour mixture. Then dip into the second and third bowls.
8. Place in the Ninja Foodi basket. Seal the lid and choose air crisp function.
9. Cook at 400 degrees for 10 minutes.

Serving Suggestion: Serve with tartar sauce.

Tip: Sprinkle with salt and pepper before serving.

Nutrition:

Calories 312, Total Fat 10.8g, Saturated Fat 2.4g, Cholesterol 101mg, Sodium 191mg, Total Carbohydrate 28.1g, Dietary Fiber 3.1g, Total Sugars 1.9g, Protein 26.7g, Potassium 493mg

Chapter 6: Vegetarian Recipes

Tender Salsa

Prep Time: 7 minutes

Cooking time: 10 minutes

Servings: 5

Ingredients:

- 1 cup tomatoes
- 1 teaspoon cumin
- 1 teaspoon ground coriander
- 1 tablespoon cilantro
- ½ cup fresh parsley
- 1 lime
- 1 sweet green pepper
- 1 red onion
- 1 teaspoon garlic powder
- 1 teaspoon olive oil
- 5 garlic cloves

Directions:

1. Remove the seeds from the sweet green pepper and cut it in half. Peel the onion and garlic cloves.

2. Place the vegetables in the pressure cooker and sprinkle them with the ½ teaspoon of olive oil. Close the lid, and set the pressure cooker to" Sauté" mode for 10 minutes. Meanwhile, chop the tomatoes and fresh parsley.

3. Peel the lime and squeeze the juice from it. Combine the lime juice with the chopped parsley, cilantro, ground coriander, and garlic powder and stir well.

4. Sprinkle the chopped tomatoes with the lime mixture. Remove the vegetables from the pressure cooker.

5. Rough chop the bell pepper and onions and add the ingredients to the tomato mixture. Mix well and serve.

Nutrition:

calories 38, fat 1.2, fiber 1, carbs 6.86, protein 1

Parmesan Tomatoes

Prep Time: 7 minutes

Cooking time: 7 minutes

Servings: 5

Ingredients:

- 10 ounces big tomatoes
- 7 ounces Parmesan cheese
- ½ teaspoon paprika
- 3 tablespoons olive oil
- 1 tablespoon basil
- 1 teaspoon cilantro
- 1 teaspoon onion powder

Directions:

1. Wash the tomatoes and slice them into the thick slices. Spray the pressure cooker with the olive oil inside.

2. Transfer the tomato slices in the pressure cooker. Combine the paprika, basil, and cilantro together and mix well. Grate the Parmesan cheese and sprinkle the tomato slices with the cheese and spice mixture.

3. Close the pressure cooker lid and cook on the" Sauté" mode for 7 minutes. When the cooking time ends, open the pressure cooker lid and let the tomatoes rest briefly. Transfer the dish to the serving plate.

Nutrition:

calories 250, fat 19.3, fiber 1, carbs 7.85, protein 12

Mushroom and Pepper Quinoa

Time: 40 minutes

Servings: 2

Ingredients:

- 1 ½ cups of quinoa (uncooked)
- 1 large onion (chopped)
- 2 cups of mushrooms (sliced)
- ½ tsp of chili flakes
- 2 medium green peppers (chopped)
- 2 tsp of minced garlic
- 2 tbsp of soy sauce

- 2 tbsp of raw brown miso paste
- 1 tbsp of tomato paste
- 2 tbsp of fresh lemon juice
- 1 ½ cups of vegetable stock
- Pinch of salt and pepper to taste

Directions:

1. Soak your quinoa thoroughly in water with a pinch of salt for 15-20 minutes. Rinse the quinoa well afterward and set aside.

2. In your pressure cooker cooking pot, add your chopped onions, mushrooms, chili flakes, green peppers, pepper and salt. Stir gently to mix everything together. Add the quinoa and the remaining ingredients.

3. Seal the lid of your pressure cooker, then set the pressure to high and set the timer for 7 minutes. Press start. When the timer is up, allow the pressure cooker to have a natural pressure release for 10 minutes, then use the quick release valve to release any remaining pressure in the pot. Carefully open the lid of the pot.

4. Give the quinoa a stir, then serve on separate plates with a fresh green salad with loads of vibrant colors.

Turmeric Rice

Prep Time: 10 minutes

Cooking time: 5 minutes

Servings: 2

Ingredients:

- 1 cup cauliflower
- 1 tablespoon turmeric
- ½ teaspoon onion powder
- ½ teaspoon garlic powder
- 1 teaspoon dried dill
- ½ teaspoon salt
- 1 teaspoon butter
- 2 pecans, chopped
- ½ cup of water

Directions:

1. Chop the cauliflower roughly and place it in the food processor. Pulse it for 3-4 time or until you get cauliflower rice.

2. After this, transfer the vegetables in the cooker. Add onion powder, garlic powder, dried dill, and salt. Then add chopped pecans and water.

3. Stir the mixture gently with the help of the spoon and close the lid. Cook it on High-pressure mode for 5 minutes.

4. Then use quick pressure release and open the lid. Drain the water using the colander. Transfer the cauliflower rice in the big bowl, add turmeric and butter. Mix up the mixture well. Serve it warm.

Nutrition:

calories 145, fat 12.3, fiber 3.6, carbs 8.1, protein 3.1

Red Bean Stew

Time: 1 hour
Servings: 4
Ingredients:

- 1 pound of red beans (dried)
- 6 cups of vegetable broth
- 2 tbsp olive oil
- 1 large onion (chopped)
- 1 large green pepper (chopped)
- 4 tsp of minced garlic
- 1 tsp of dried thyme
- 1 cup of celery stalks (chopped)
- 1 tsp of dried oregano
- 1 bay leaf
- 1/2 tbsp of ground paprika
- 1/2 tsp of ground cayenne pepper
- 6 cups cooked white or brown rice
- Pinch of salt and pepper to taste

Directions:

1. In a medium-sized frying pan, sauté your onions, green pepper, celery, and garlic in olive oil until the onions are translucent. Then scrape the onion mixer into the bottom of your pressure cooker cooking pot.
2. Add your red beans (do not presoak them), vegetable broth, and all remaining spices.
3. Seal the lid of your pressure cooker and set your pressure to high pressure and set the timer for 50 minutes, then press start. Once the timer is up, allow the pressure cooker to naturally release the pressure for 10 minutes, then use the quick release valve to remove any remaining pressure.
4. Open the lid of the pressure cooker carefully, then use a potato masher to mash the bean mixer roughly. This should give a chunky consistency. Serve with cooked rice.

Zucchini Noodles

Prep Time: 10 minutes

Cooking time: 10 minutes

Servings: 6

Ingredients:

- 2 medium green zucchini
- 1 tablespoon wine vinegar
- 1 teaspoon white pepper
- ½ teaspoon cilantro
- ¼ teaspoon nutmeg
- 1 cup chicken stock
- 1 garlic clove

Directions:

1. Wash the zucchini and use a spiralizer to make the zucchini noodles.
2. Peel the garlic and chop it. Combine the cilantro, chopped garlic clove, nutmeg, and white pepper together in a mixing bowl.
3. Sprinkle the zucchini noodles with the spice mixture. Pour the chicken stock in the pressure cooker and sauté the liquid on the manual mode until it is become to boil.
4. Add the zucchini noodles and wine vinegar and stir the mixture gently.
5. Cook for 3 minutes on the" Sauté" mode.
6. Remove the zucchini noodles from the pressure cooker and serve.

Nutrition:

calories 28, fat 0.7, fiber 1, carbs 3.94, protein 2

Refried Beans

Time: 50 minutes

Servings: 6

Ingredients:

- 1 pound of pinto beans
- 1 large onion (diced)
- 4 tsp of minced garlic
- 4 cups of vegetable broth
- 1 tsp of ground cumin
- 1 tsp of dried oregano

- 1 tsp of chili powder
- 2 stalks of green onions (diced)
- 1 cup of grated cheddar cheese
- Pinch of salt and pepper to taste

Directions:

1. Inside the cooking pot of your pressure cooker, add your onions, chili powder, drained pinto beans, ground cumin, dried oregano and minced garlic, then add your vegetable broth.
2. Spicy Tip: You can add an extra ½ tsp of chili powder or chili flakes if you would like some super spiced beans.
3. Give your ingredients a quick mix through and seal the lid of your pressure cooker. Set your pressure to high pressure and set your timer for 40 minutes, then press start. Once the timer is up, allow the pressure cooker to do a natural release of pressure for 10 minutes, then use the quick pressure release valve to release any remaining pressure thereafter. Carefully remove the lid, avoiding the steam.
4. Strain the beans from the pot and keep the liquid leftover to one side, put your beans back in the pot and use a potato masher to mash your beans to your desired consistency. This will result in a more chunkier bean mix, alternatively you may use a hand-blender to get a smoother consistency.
5. Season your bean mix with a pinch of salt and pepper, then slowly add your beans liquid back into your mashed beans until you have achieved the consistency that you desire.
6. Sprinkle over your green onions and cheese on top of your beans and dish up while it is hot.

Spicy Chinese Green Beans

Prep Time: 10 minutes

Cooking time: 15 minutes

Servings: 8

Ingredients:

- 12 ounces green beans
- 1 teaspoon garlic powder
- 1 teaspoon onion powder
- 4 garlic cloves
- 2 tablespoons olive oil
- 1 teaspoon cayenne pepper
- 1 jalapeno pepper
- 1 teaspoon butter
- ½ teaspoon salt
- 1 cup of water

Directions:

1. Wash the green beans and cut each into two equal parts.
2. Toss the green beans in the mixing bowl.
3. Sprinkle the vegetables with the onion powder, chili pepper, and salt and stir. Remove the seeds from the jalapeno pepper and chop it into tiny pieces.
4. Add the chopped jalapeno1 in the green beans mixture. Peel the garlic and slice it. Combine the sliced garlic with the olive oil. Blend the mixture and transfer it to the pressure cooker. Add the water and stir.
5. Put the green beans in the pressure cooker and close the lid.
6. Set the pressure cooker mode to" Sauté," and cook the vegetables for 15 minutes. When the dish is cooked, you should have firm but not crunchy green beans.
7. Remove the green beans from the pressure cooker and discard the liquid before serving.

Nutrition:

calories 49, fat 4.1, fiber 1, carbs 3, protein 1

Veggie Frittata

Time: 30 minutes

Servings: 8

Ingredients:

- 8 eggs
- 1/4 cup of onion (chopped)
- 1 tsp of minced garlic
- 1/4 cup of green pepper(chopped)
- 2 cups of shredded kale
- 2 cups of mushrooms (sliced)
- 1 cup of grated mozzarella cheese
- chives for garnishing
- 2 large tomatoes (chopped)
- Pinch of salt and pepper to taste

Directions:

1. Pour 1 cup of water into the bottom of your pressure cooker cooking pot. Then place your reversible wire rack inside the pot above the water.
2. Spray a silicone cake pan with nonstick cooking spray.
3. In a medium-sized mixing bowl, add your onion, garlic, green pepper, kale, mushrooms and half of your mozzarella cheese and mixed gently, then transfer the ingredients into the bottom of your silicone pan.

4. Then whisk all your eggs together and pour them directly over the vegetable mix in the pan.
5. Gently lower your silicone pan onto the reversible wire rack inside your pot and seal the lid. Set your pressure to high and set the timer for 10 minutes. Press start.
6. Once the timer is up, allow the pressure to naturally release for 10 minutes, then use the quick release valve to release any remaining pressure in the pot. Open the lid carefully and pull out your silicone pan.
7. Tip the frittata upside down onto a serving plate and top with chopped tomatoes, chives and the remaining mozzarella cheese. Serve while hot.

Mexican Style Quinoa

Time: 25 minutes

Servings: 2

Ingredients:

- 1 cup of water
- 1 cup of quinoa (rinsed and drained)
- 1 cup of frozen peas
- 1 cup of corn kernels
- 15 oz can of black beans (drained and rinsed)
- 1 red pepper (diced)
- 2 green onions (sliced)

Toppings: chopped cilantro and lime slices

Directions:

1. Add water to the bottom of your pressure cooker cooking pot, then add the quinoa, frozen peas, corn kernels, black beans, red pepper and green onions.
2. Seal the lid of your pressure cooker and set the pressure to high and the timer for 3 minutes. Press start.
3. Once the timer is up, allow the pressure to release naturally until completely depressurized. This can take 15 to 20 minutes to complete, then remove the lid.
4. Serve in separate bowls and add your chopped cilantro and lime slices on top.

Quinoa health bowl

Time: 25 minutes (excluding soaking)

Servings: 6

Ingredients:

- 1 ½ cups of quinoa (soaked in water for 1 hour)
- 1 can of coconut milk (15 ounce)
- 1 ⅕ cups of water

- 1 cup of fresh fruit
- ¼ cup of coconut flakes
- 2 tsp vanilla extract
- ¼ cup of maple syrup
- 1 tsp ground cinnamon

Directions:

1. Drain the excess water from your soaked quinoa, then rinse it thoroughly.
2. Put your quinoa into the cooking pot of your pressure cooker, then add the coconut milk, water, vanilla extract, maple syrup and cinnamon.
3. Seal the lid and set your pressure cooker to low pressure for 12 minutes.
4. Allow the pressure to release naturally for 10 minutes, then use the quick release valve for the remaining pressure.
5. Scoop the quinoa into separate bowls, and add fresh fruit and coconut flakes to give your health bowl some oomph! Enjoy!

Bok Choy with Mustard Sauce

Prep Time: 10 minutes

Cooking time: 12 minutes

Servings: 7

Ingredients:

- 1 pound bok choy
- 1 cup of water
- ⅓ cup of soy sauce
- 1 teaspoon salt
- 1 teaspoon red chili flakes
- 5 tablespoon mustard
- ⅓ cup cream
- 1 teaspoon cumin seeds
- 1 teaspoon ground black pepper
- 1 tablespoon butter
- ¼ cup garlic clove

Directions:

1. Wash the bok choy and chop it into pieces. Combine water, soy sauce, salt, chili flakes, cumin seeds, and ground black pepper together.
2. Blend the mixture. Peel the garlic clove and cut into thin slices. Add the butter in the pressure cooker and sliced garlic.

3. Set the pressure cooker to" Sauté" mode and sauté for 1 minute. Add the cream, soy sauce mixture, and bok choy. Close the lid. Set the pot to «Sauté» mode and cook for 10 minutes.

4. Drain the water from the pressure cooker and sprinkle the bok choy with the mustard, stirring well.

5. Cook for 2 minutes on the manual mode, then transfer the dish to the serving plate immediately.

Nutrition:

calories 83, fat 4.8, fiber 2.1, carbs 7.4, protein 4.2

Romano Cheese Zucchini Circles

Prep Time: 10 minutes

Cooking time: 30 minutes

Servings: 6

Ingredients:

- 1 pound yellow zucchini
- 3 tablespoons minced garlic
- ½ cup coconut flour
- 3 tablespoons olive oil
- 3 eggs
- ¼ cup of coconut milk
- 7 ounces Romano cheese
- 1 teaspoon salt

Directions:

1. Wash the zucchini and slice them. Combine the minced garlic and salt together and stir the mixture.

2. Combine the minced garlic mixture and zucchini slices together and mix well.

3. Add the eggs in the mixing bowl and whisk the mixture. Add coconut milk and coconut flour. Stir it carefully until combined. Grate the Romano cheese and add it to the egg mixture and mix.

4. Pour the olive oil in the pressure cooker and preheat it. Dip the sliced zucchini in the egg mixture.

5. Transfer the dipped zucchini in the pressure cooker and cook the dish on the" Sauté" mode for 2 minutes on each side.

6. When the dish is cooked, remove it from the pressure cooker, drain any excess fat using a paper towel, and serve.

Nutrition:

calories 301, fat 21.6, fiber 5.1, carbs 12.5, protein 16

Spiced Veggie Lo Mein

Time: 15 minutes

Servings: 6

Ingredients:

- 1 tsp of minced garlic
- 8 oz linguine or fettuccine pasta (break them in half)
- 1 cup of frozen peas
- 2 cups of broccoli florets
- 1 1/2 cups of chicken broth
- 2 carrots (sliced julienne style)
- 1 tsp of grated ginger
- 2 tbsp of soy sauce
- 1 tbsp of rice wine
- 1 tbsp of brown sugar
- 1 tbsp of ground paprika
- 1 tbsp of oyster sauce

Directions:

1. In the cooking pot of your pressure cooker, add the minced garlic, peas, broccoli, carrots, and your pasta of choice.
2. Then in a large bowl, add your broth, ginger, soy sauce, ground paprika, oyster sauce, brown sugar and rice wine vinegar. Gently whisk the liquids and spices together with a hand whisk and pour it over the vegetables and pasta inside the pressure cooker
3. Seal the lid of your pressure cooker, set your pressure to high and set the timer for 5 minutes, then press start.
4. When the timer is up, use the quick release valve to carefully release all the pressure from your pot as fast as possible. You do not want the pressure to release naturally as this will result in overcooked, mushy pasta.
5. Lift the lid carefully and stir the mix gently to break up the strands of pasta into the sauce. it should thicken slightly as you stir.
6. Serve immediately while hot for the best taste experience that you can get!

Black Bean Chili

Time: 50 minutes (excluding soaking time)

Servings: 6

Ingredients:

- 1 pound of dried black beans
- 2 red peppers (chopped)
- 1 large onion (chopped)
- 1 large carrot (chopped)
- ½ tbsp of salt
- 2 tbsp of chili powder
- 1 tsp of ground paprika
- 1 tbsp of cumin
- 2 tbsp of tomato paste
- 4 garlic cloves (minced)
- 8 oz packet of tomato sauce
- 3 large tomatoes (chopped)
- 3 cups of water
- 2 cups of fresh corn kernels

Directions:

1. First, pour your black beans into a large-sized container and completely cover them in boiling water for 3 hours. Once thoroughly soaked, drain and rinse them off, then add them into the pressure cooker cooking pot.

2. Add red peppers, chopped onion, chopped carrot, salt, chili powder, ground paprika, cumin, tomato paste, tomato sauce, chopped tomatoes, garlic and water all into the pressure cooker on top of the black beans. Seal the lid, set the pressure to high and set your timer for 40 minutes.

3. Once the timer is up, allow your pressure cooker to release pressure naturally for 10 minutes, then use your quick release valve to release the last of the pressure.

4. Carefully remove the lid and stir in the corn. Allow to sit for a further 5 minutes, then serve with a sprig of parsley and tortilla chips.

Pickled Garlic

Prep Time: 10 minutes

Cooking time: 9 minutes

Servings: 12

Ingredients:

- 2 cups garlic
- 1 tablespoon salt
- 1 tablespoon olive oil
- 1 teaspoon fennel seeds
- ½ teaspoon black peas
- 3 cups of water
- 5 tablespoon apple cider vinegar
- 1 teaspoon lemon juice
- 1 teaspoon lemon zest
- 1 tablespoon stevia
- 1 teaspoon red chili flakes

Directions:

Place the salt, olive oil. Fennel seeds, black peas, lemon juice, lemon zest, stevia, and chili flakes in the pressure cooker. Add water and stir it.

Preheat the liquid on the" Pressure" mode for 5 minutes. Meanwhile, peel the garlic. Put the garlic into the preheated liquid. Add apple cider vinegar and stir the mixture. Close the lid and cook the garlic on the" Pressure" mode for 4 minutes.

Open the pressure cooker lid and leave the garlic in the liquid for 7 minutes, Transfer the garlic to the liquid into a glass jar, such as a Mason jar. Seal the jar tightly and keep it in your refrigerator for at least 1 day before serving.

Nutrition:

calories 46, fat 1.3, fiber 0.6, carbs 7.7, protein 1.5

Curried Chickpeas

Time: 30 minutes (excluding soaking)

Servings: 4

Ingredients:

- 1.5 cups of chickpeas (Presoak for 8 hours)
- 1 8oz can of tomatoes (Peeled and chopped)
- ½ cup of chopped red onion
- 2 garlic cloves (chopped)
- ½ tsp of chilli powder
- ½ tsp of masala powder
- ½ tsp of turmeric
- 1 tbsp of curry powder
- 2 tbsp of lemon juice
- 2 bay leaves
- 1 ½ cups of water
- Pinch of salt and pepper to taste

Directions:

1. Rinse the pre-soaked chickpeas thoroughly with cold water, then put them into your pressure cooker cooking pot along with the extra water, tomatoes, onions, garlic, spices, lemon juice and bay leaves.
2. Give a light stir to mix everything together and seal the lid of the pot.
3. Set your pressure to high, and set the timer for 15 minutes, then press start.
4. Once the timer is up, allow the pressure cooker to naturally release pressure for 10 minutes, then use the quick release valve to release the rest of the pressure.
5. Open the lid carefully and give your chickpeas a final stir, then serve over rice or with naan bread.

Cloud Bread

Prep Time: 15 minutes

Cooking time: 7 minutes

Servings: 4

Ingredients:

- 1 egg
- ¾ teaspoon cream of tartar
- 1 tablespoon cream cheese
- ¾ teaspoon onion powder
- ¾ teaspoon dried cilantro

Directions:

1. Separate the egg white and egg yolk and place them into the separated bowls. Whisk the egg white with the cream of tartar until the strong peaks.

2. After this, whisk the cream cheese with the egg white until fluffy. Add onion powder and dried cilantro. Stir gently.

3. After this, carefully add egg white and stir it. Scoop the mixture into the Ninja cooker to get small "clouds" and lower the crisp lid.

4. Cook the bread for 7 minutes at 360 F or until it is light brown. Chill little before serving.

Nutrition:

calories 27, fat 0.2, fiber 0, carbs 0.9, protein 1.6

Spiced Lentil Stew

Time: 40 minutes

Servings: 4

Ingredients:

- 1 cup of split red lentils
- 2 medium potatoes (peeled and chopped)
- 4 carrots (peeled and chopped)
- 1 medium red onion (diced)
- 1 tsp of fresh grated ginger
- 3 tsp of minced garlic
- 1 tsp of chili powder
- 1 tsp of salt
- 2-3 cups water divided
- 1/2 a lime

Directions:

1. In your pressure cooker cooking pot, add your lentils, potatoes, carrots, red onion, ginger, garlic, chili powder, salt and water.

2. Seal the lip of the pressure cooker and set the pressure to high, then set the timer for 20 minutes and press start.

3. Once the timer is up, allow your stew to sit while the pressure releases naturally for 15 minutes. Finish off with opening the quick release valve for any remaining pressure to be released, then open the lid carefully.

4. Add more water to the stew if a runny consistency is preferred. Give the stew a final stir and squeeze your fresh lime juice into the stew before serving.

Sweet Tomato Salsa

Prep Time: 10 minutes

Cooking time: 8 minutes

Servings: 6

Ingredients:

- 2 cups tomatoes
- 1 teaspoon sugar
- ⅓ cup fresh cilantro
- 2 white onions
- 1 teaspoon ground black pepper
- 1 teaspoon cayenne pepper
- ½ jalapeno pepper
- 1 teaspoon olive oil
- 1 tablespoon minced garlic
- ⅓ cup of green olives
- 1 teaspoon paprika
- ⅓ cup basil
- 1 tablespoon Erythritol

Directions:

1. Peel the onions and remove the seeds from the jalapeno pepper. Transfer the vegetables to the pressure cooker and sprinkle them with the olive oil. Close the lid and cook the ingredients on the" Steam" mode for 8 minutes.
2. Meanwhile, wash the tomatoes and chop them. Place the chopped tomatoes in the bowl. Chop the cilantro. Add the chopped cilantro, ground black pepper, chili pepper, and minced garlic in the chopped tomatoes. Add green olives, chop them or leave them whole as desired. Chop the basil and add it to the salsa mixture. Add paprika and olive oil.
3. When the vegetables are cooked, remove them from the pressure cooker and chill.
4. Chop the vegetables and add them to the salsa mixture. Sprinkle the dish with Erythritol. Mix well and serve.

Nutrition:

calories 41, fat 1.1, fiber 1.9, carbs 7.7, protein 1.2

Asparagus Mash

Prep Time: 6 minutes

Cooking time: 6 minutes

Servings: 1

Ingredients:

- ½ cup asparagus
- ½ cup of water
- 1 tablespoon heavy cream
- 1 tablespoon fresh basil, chopped
- ½ teaspoon salt
- ¾ teaspoon lemon juice

Directions:

1. Put asparagus in the Ninja cooker. Add water and salt. Close and seal the lid.
2. Cook the vegetables on High-pressure mode for 6 minutes (use quick pressure release).
3. Open the lid and drain half of the liquid. Add fresh basil.
4. Using the hand blender, blend the mixture until smooth. Then add lemon juice and heavy cream. Stir the mash and transfer it into the serving bowls.

Nutrition:

calories 67, fat 5.7, fiber 1.5, carbs 3.2, protein 1.9

Seasoned Eggs

Prep Time: 15 minutes

Cooking time: 5 minutes

Servings: 7

Ingredients:

- 1 tablespoon mustard
- ¼ cup cream
- 1 teaspoon salt
- 8 eggs
- 1 teaspoon mayonnaise
- ¼ cup dill
- 1 teaspoon ground white pepper
- 1 teaspoon minced garlic

Directions:

1. Put the eggs in the pressure cooker and add water. Cook the eggs at the high pressure for 5 minutes.

2. Remove the eggs from the pressure cooker and chill. Peel the eggs and cut them in half. Remove the egg yolks and mash them.

3. Add the mustard, cream, salt, mayonnaise, ground white pepper, and minced garlic to the mashed egg yolks.

4. Chop the dill and sprinkle the egg yolk mixture with the dill. Mix well until smooth. Transfer the egg yolk mixture to a pastry bag and fill the egg whites with the yolk mixture. Serve immediately.

Nutrition:

calories 170, fat 12.8, fiber 0, carbs 2.42, protein 11

Chapter 7: Dessert Recipes

Double Chocolate Cake

Prep Time: 15 minutes

Cooking time: 1 hour

Servings: 12

Ingredients:

- ½ cup coconut flour
- 1½ cups Erythritol, divided
- 5 tablespoons cacao powder, divided
- 1 teaspoon organic baking powder
- ½ teaspoon salt
- 3 organic eggs
- 3 organic egg yolks
- ½ cup butter, melted and cooled
- 1 teaspoon organic vanilla extract
- ½ teaspoon liquid stevia
- 4 ounces 70% dark chocolate chips
- 2 cups hot water

Directions:

1. Grease the pot of Ninja Foodi.
2. In a large bowl, add the flour, 1¼ cups of Erythritol, 3 tablespoons of cacao powder, baking powder and salt.
3. In another bowl, add the eggs, egg yolks, butter, vanilla extract and liquid stevia and beat until well combined.
4. Add the egg mixture into flour mixture and mix until just combined.
5. In a small bowl, add hot water, remaining cacao powder and Erythritol and beat until well combined.
6. In the prepared pot of Ninja Foodi, place the mixture evenly and top with chocolate chips, followed by the water mixture.
7. Close the Ninja Foodi with crisping lid and select "Slow Cooker".
8. Set on "Low" for 3 hours.
9. Press "Start/Stop" to begin cooking.
10. Transfer the pan onto a wire rack to cool for about 10 minutes.
11. Carefully invert the cake onto the wire rack to cool completely.
12. Cut into desired-sized slices and serve.

Nutrition:

Calories: 169, Fats: 15.4g, Net Carbs: 2.3g, Carbs: 4.4g, Fiber: 2.1g, Sugar: 0.2g, Proteins: 3.9g, Sodium: 174mg

Chocolate Cheesecake

Prep Time: 15 minutes, Cooking time: 20 minutes, Servings: 10

Ingredients:

For Crust:
- ¼ cup coconut flour
- ¼ cup almond flour
- 2½ tablespoons cacao powder
- 1½ tablespoons Erythritol
- 2 tablespoons butter, melted

For Filling:
- 16 ounces cream cheese, softened
- 1/3 cup cacao powder
- ½ teaspoon powdered Erythritol
- ½ teaspoon stevia powder
- 1 large organic egg
- 2 large organic egg yolks
- 6 ounces unsweetened dark chocolate, melted
- ¾ cup heavy cream
- ¼ cup sour cream
- 1 teaspoon organic vanilla extract

Directions:

1. For crust: in a bowl, mix together flours, cacao powder and Erythritol.
2. Add the butter and mix until well combined.
3. Place the mixture into a parchment paper lined 7-inch springform pan evenly and with your fingers, press evenly.
4. For filling: in a food processor, add the cream cheese, cacao powder, monk fruit powder and stevia and pulse until smooth.
5. Add the egg and egg yolks and pulse until well combined.
6. Add the remaining ingredients and pulse until well combined.
7. Place the filling mixture on top of crust evenly and with a rubber spatula, smooth the surface.
8. With a piece of foil, cover the springform pan loosely.
9. In the pot of Ninja Foodi, place 2 cups of water.
10. Arrange a "Reversible Rack" in the pot of Ninja Foodi.
11. Place the springform pan over the "Reversible Rack".
12. Close the Ninja Foodi with pressure lid and place the pressure valve to "Seal" position.
13. Select "Pressure" and set to "High" for 20 minutes.
14. Press "Start/Stop" to begin cooking.
15. Switch the valve to "Vent" and do a "Natural" release.
16. Place the pan onto a wire rack to cool completely.
17. Refrigerate for about 6-8 hours before serving.

Nutrition:

Calories: 385, Fats: 35.6g, Net Carbs: 5.6g, Carbs: 9.8g, Fiber: 4.2g, Sugar: 0.4g, Proteins: 8.9g, Sodium: 172mg

Lemon Cheesecake

Prep Time: 15 minutes
Cooking time: 4 hours
Servings: 12

Ingredients:

For Crust:
- 1½ cups almond flour
- 4 tablespoons butter, melted
- 3 tablespoons sugar-free peanut butter
- 3 tablespoons Erythritol
- 1 large organic egg, beaten

For Filling:
- 1 cup ricotta cheese
- 24 ounces cream cheese, softened
- 1½ cups Erythritol
- 2 teaspoons liquid stevia
- 1/3 cup heavy cream
- 2 large organic eggs
- 3 large organic egg yolks
- 1 tablespoon fresh lemon juice
- 1 tablespoon organic vanilla extract

Directions:

1. Grease the pot of Ninja Foodi.
2. For crust: in a bowl, add all the ingredients and mix until well combined.
3. In the pot of prepared of Ninja Foodi, place the crust mixture and press to smooth the top surface.
4. With a fork, prick the crust at many places.
5. For filling: in a food processor, add the ricotta cheese and pulse until smooth.
6. In a large bowl, add the ricotta, cream cheese, Erythritol and stevia and with an electric mixer, beat over medium speed until smooth.
7. In another bowl, add the heavy cream, eggs, egg yolks, lemon juice and vanilla extract and beat until well combined.
8. Add the egg mixture into cream cheese mixture and beat over medium speed until just combined.
9. Place the filling mixture over crust evenly.
10. Close the Ninja Foodi with crisping lid and select "Slow Cooker".
11. Set on "Low" for 3-4 hours.
12. Press "Start/Stop" to begin cooking.
13. Place the pan onto a wire racks to cool.
14. Refrigerate to chill for at least 6-8 hours before serving.

Nutrition:

Calories: 410, Fats: 37.9g, Net Carbs: 5.1g, Carbs: 6.9g, Fiber: 1.8g, Sugar: 1.3g, Proteins: 13g, Sodium: 260mg

Vanilla Cheesecake

Prep Time: 15 minutes
Cooking time: 2 hours
Servings: 6

Ingredients:

For Crust:
- 1 cup almonds, toasted
- 1 organic egg
- 2 tablespoons butter
- 4-6 drops liquid stevia

For Filling:
- 2 (8-ounce packages cream cheese, softened
- 4 tablespoons heavy cream
- 2 organic eggs
- 1 tablespoon coconut flour
- 1 teaspoon liquid stevia
- 1 teaspoon organic vanilla extract

Directions:

1. For crust: in a high-speed food processor, add almonds and pulse until a flour like consistency is achieved.
2. In a bowl, add ground almond, egg, butter and stevia and mix until well combined.
3. In the bottom of a 1½-quart oval pan, place the crust mixture and press to smooth the top surface, leaving a little room on each side.
4. For filling: in a bowl, add all ingredients and with an immersion blender, blend until well combined.
5. Place the filling mixture over crust evenly.
6. In the pot of Ninja Foodi, place 1 cup of water.
7. Carefully, arrange the pan in the pot of Ninja Foodi.
8. Close the Ninja Foodi with crisping lid and select "Slow Cooker".
9. Set on "Low" for 2 hours.
10. Press "Start/Stop" to begin cooking.
11. Place the pan onto a wire racks to cool.
12. Refrigerate to chill for at least 6-8 hours before serving.

Nutrition:

Calories: 446, Fats: 42.9g, Net Carbs: 4.4g, Carbs: 7.2g, Fiber: 2.8g, Sugar: 1.1g, Proteins: 10.6g, Sodium: 270mg

Chocolate Walnut Cake

Prep Time: 15 minutes

Cooking time: 20 minutes

Servings: 6

Ingredients:

- 3 organic eggs
- 1 cup almond flour
- 2/3 cup Erythritol
- 1/3 cup heavy whipping cream
- ¼ cup butter, softened
- ¼ cup cacao powder
- ¼ cup walnuts, chopped
- 1 teaspoon organic baking powder

Directions:

1. In a large bowl, add all the ingredients and with a mixer, beat until fluffy.
2. Place the mixture into a greased Bundt pan.
3. With a piece of foil, cover the pan.
4. In the pot of Ninja Foodi, place 2 cups of water.
5. Arrange a "Reversible Rack" in the pot of Ninja Foodi.
6. Place the Bundt pan over the "Reversible Rack".
7. Close the Ninja Foodi with pressure lid and place the pressure valve to "Seal" position.
8. Select "Pressure" and set to "High" for 20 minutes.
9. Press "Start/Stop" to begin cooking.
10. Switch the valve to "Vent" and do a "Quick" release.
11. Place the pan onto a wire rack to cool for about 10 minutes.
12. Carefully invert the cake onto the wire rack to cool completely.
13. Cut into desired-sized slices and serve.

Nutrition:

Calories: 270, Fats: 25.4g, Net Carbs: 3.6g, Carbs: 7g, Fiber: 3.4g, Sugar: 0.9g, Proteins: 8.9g, Sodium: 89mg

Chocolate Blackberry Cake

Prep Time: 15 minutes

Cooking time: 3 hours

Servings: 10

Ingredients:

- 2 cups almond flour
- 1 cup unsweetened coconut, shredded
- ½ cup Erythritol
- ¼ cup unsweetened protein powder
- 2 teaspoons baking soda
- ¼ teaspoon salt
- 4 large organic eggs
- ½ cup heavy cream
- ½ cup unsalted butter, melted
- 1 cup fresh blackberries
- 1/3 cup 70% dark chocolate chips

Directions:

1. Grease the pot of Ninja Foodi.
2. In a bowl, mix together the flour, coconut, Erythritol, protein powder, baking soda and salt.
3. In another large bowl, add the eggs, cream and butter and beat until well combined.
4. Add the flour mixture and mix until well combined.
5. Fold in the blackberries and chocolate chips.
6. In the prepared pot of Ninja Foodi, place the mixture.
7. Close the Ninja Foodi with crisping lid and select "Slow Cooker".
8. Set on "Low" for 3 hours.
9. Press "Start/Stop" to begin cooking.
10. Transfer the pan onto a wire rack to cool for about 10 minutes.
11. Carefully invert the cake onto the wire rack to cool completely.
12. Cut into desired-sized slices and serve.

Nutrition:

Calories: 305, Fats: 27.5g, Net Carbs: 3.8g, Carbs: 7.7g, Fiber: 3.9g, Sugar: 2.2g, Proteins: 10.6g, Sodium: 434mg

Strawberry Crumble

Prep Time: 15 minutes

Cooking time: 2 hours

Servings: 5

Ingredients:

- 1 cup almond flour
- 2 tablespoons butter, melted
- 8-10 drops liquid stevia
- 3-4 cups fresh strawberries, hulled and sliced
- 1 tablespoon butter, chopped

Directions:

1. Lightly, grease the pot of Ninja Foodi.
2. In a bowl, add the flour, melted butter and stevia and mix until a crumbly mixture forms.
3. In the pot of the prepared Ninja Foodi, place the strawberry slices and dot with chopped butter.
4. Spread the flour mixture on top evenly
5. Close the Ninja Foodi with crisping lid and select "Slow Cooker".
6. Set on "Low" for 2 hours.
7. Press "Start/Stop" to begin cooking.
8. Place the pan onto a wire racks to cool slightly.
9. Serve warm.

Nutrition:

Calories: 233, Fats: 19.2g, Net Carbs: 6.6g, Carbs: 10.7g, Fiber: 4.1g, Sugar: 5g, Proteins: 0.7g, Sodium: 50mg

Mini Chocolate Cheesecakes

Prep Time: 15 minutes

Cooking time: 18 minutes

Servings: 4

Ingredients:

- 1 organic egg
- 8 ounces cream cheese, softened
- ¼ cup Erythritol
- 1 tablespoon powdered peanut butter
- ¾ tablespoon cacao powder

Directions:

1. Grease the pot of Ninja Foodi.
2. In a blender, add the eggs and cream cheese and pulse until smooth.
3. Add the remaining ingredients and pulse until well combined.
4. Transfer the mixture into 2 (8-ounce mason jars evenly.
5. In the pot of Ninja Foodi, place 1 cup of water.
6. Arrange a "Reversible Rack" in the pot of Ninja Foodi.
7. Place the mason jars over the "Reversible Rack".
8. Close the Ninja Foodi with pressure lid and place the pressure valve to "Seal" position.
9. Select "Pressure" and set to "High" for 18 minutes.
10. Press "Start/Stop" to begin cooking.
11. Switch the valve to "Vent" and do a "Natural" release.
12. Open the lid and place the ramekins onto a wire racks to cool.
13. Refrigerate to chill for at least 6-8 hours before serving.

Nutrition:

Calories: 222, Fats: 28.4g, Net Carbs: 2.3g, Carbs: 2.9g, Fiber: 0.6g, Sugar: 0.3g, Proteins: 6.5g, Sodium: 195mg

Raspberry Cobbler

Prep Time: 15 minutes
Cooking time: 2 hours
Servings: 8

Ingredients:

- 1 cup almond flour
- ¼ cup coconut flour
- ¾ cup Erythritol
- 1 teaspoon baking soda
- ¼ teaspoon ground cinnamon
- 1/8 teaspoon salt
- ¼ cup unsweetened coconut milk
- 2 tablespoons coconut oil
- 1 large organic egg, beaten lightly
- 4 cups fresh raspberries

Directions:

1. Grease the pot of Ninja Foodi.
2. In a large bowl, mix together flours, Erythritol, baking soda, cinnamon and salt.
3. In another bowl, add the coconut milk, coconut oil and egg and beat until well combined.

4. Add the egg mixture into flour mixture and mix until just combined.
5. In the pot of the prepared Ninja Foodi, place the mixture evenly and top with raspberries.
6. Close the Ninja Foodi with crisping lid and select "Slow Cooker".
7. Set on "Low" for 2 hours.
8. Press "Start/Stop" to begin cooking.
9. Place the pan onto a wire racks to cool slightly.
10. Serve warm.

Nutrition:

Calories: 164, Fats: 12.5g, Net Carbs: 5.2g, Carbs: 10.9g, Fiber: 5.7g, Sugar: 3.5g, Proteins: 4.7g, Sodium: 206mg

Mini Vanilla Cheesecakes

Prep Time: 15 minutes
Cooking time: 10 minutes
Servings: 2

Ingredients:

- ¾ cup Erythritol
- 2 organic eggs
- 1 teaspoon organic vanilla extract
- ½ teaspoon fresh lemon juice
- 16 ounces cream cheese, softened
- 2 tablespoon sour cream

Directions:

1. Arrange the "Cook & Crisp Basket" in the pot of Ninja Foodi.
2. Close the Ninja Foodi with crisping lid and select "Air Crisp".
3. Set the temperature to 350 degrees F for 5 minutes.
4. Press "Start/Stop" to begin preheating.
5. In a blender, add the Erythritol, eggs, vanilla extract and lemon juice and pulse until smooth.
6. Add the cream cheese and sour cream and pulse until smooth.
7. Place the mixture into 2 (4-inch springform pans evenly.
8. After preheating, open the lid.
9. Place the pans into the "Cook & Crisp Basket".
10. Close the Ninja Foodi with crisping lid and select "Air Crisp".
11. Set the temperature to 350 degrees for 10 minutes.
12. Press "Start/Stop" to begin cooking.
13. Place the pans onto a wire rack to cool.
14. Refrigerator overnight before serving.

Nutrition:

Calories: 886, Fats: 86g, Net Carbs: 7.2g, Carbs: 7.2g, Fiber: 0g, Sugar: 1.1g, Proteins: 23.1g, Sodium: 740mg

Yogurt Cheesecake

Prep Time: 10 minutes

Cooking time: 40 minutes

Servings: 8

Ingredients:

- 4 cups plain Greek Yogurt
- 1 cup Erythritol
- ½ teaspoon organic vanilla extract

Directions:

1. Line a cake pan with Parchment paper.
2. In a bowl, add the yogurt and Erythritol and with a hand mixer, mix well.
3. Add the vanilla extract and stir to combine.
4. Place the mixture into the prepared pan and cover with paper kitchen towel.
5. Then with a piece of foil, cover the pan tightly.
6. In the pot of Ninja Foodi, place 1 cup of water.
7. Arrange a "Reversible Rack" in the pot of Ninja Foodi.
8. Place the ramekins over the "Reversible Rack".
9. Close the Ninja Foodi with pressure lid and place the pressure valve to "Seal" position.
10. Select "Pressure" and set to "High" for 40 minutes.
11. Press "Start/Stop" to begin cooking.
12. Switch the valve to "Vent" and do a "Quick" release.
13. Place the pan onto a wire rack and remove the foil and paper tower.
14. Again, cover the pan with a new paper towel and refrigerate to cool overnight.

Nutrition:

Calories: 88, Fats: 1.5g, Net Carbs: 8.7g, Carbs: 8.7g, Fiber: 0g, Sugar: 8.7g, Proteins: 7g, Sodium: 86mg

Chocolate Brownie Cake

Prep Time: 15 minutes

Cooking time: 35 minutes

Servings: 6

Ingredients:

- ½ cup 70% dark chocolate chips
- ½ cup butter
- 3 organic eggs
- ¼ cup Erythritol
- 1 teaspoon organic vanilla extract

Directions:

1. In a microwave-safe bowl, add the chocolate chips and butter and microwave for about 1 minute, stirring after every 20 seconds.
2. Remove from the microwave and stir well.
3. Arrange a "Reversible Rack" in the pot of the Ninja Foodi.
4. Close the Ninja Foodi with crisping lid and select "Air Crisp".
5. Set the temperature to 350 degrees F for 5 minutes.
6. Press "Start/Stop" to begin preheating.
7. In a bowl, add the eggs, Erythritol and vanilla extract and blend until light and frothy.
8. Slowly, add the chocolate mixture and beat again until well combined.
9. Place the mixture into a lightly grease springform pan.
10. After preheating, open the lid.
11. Place the springform pan into the "Cook & Crisp Basket".
12. Close the Ninja Foodi with crisping lid and select "Air Crisp".
13. Set the temperature to 350 degrees F for 35 minutes.
14. Press "Start/Stop" to begin cooking.
15. Place the pan onto a wire rack to cool for about 10 minutes.
16. Carefully invert the cake onto the wire rack to cool completely.
17. Cut into desired-sized slices and serve.

Nutrition:

Calories: 302, Fats: 28.2g, Net Carbs: 2.9g, Carbs: 5.6g, Fiber: 2.7g, Sugar: 1.2g, Proteins: 5.6g, Sodium: 147mg

Lime Cheesecake

Prep Time: 15 minutes

Cooking time: 30 minutes

Servings: 6

Ingredients:

- ¼ cup plus 1 teaspoon Erythritol
- 8 ounces cream cheese, softened
- 1/3 cup Ricotta cheese
- 1 teaspoon fresh lime zest, grated
- 2 tablespoons fresh lime juice
- ½ teaspoon organic vanilla extract
- 2 organic eggs
- 2 tablespoons sour cream

Directions:

1. In a bowl, add ¼ cup of Erythritol and remaining ingredients except eggs and sour cream and with a hand mixer, beat on high speed until smooth.
2. Add the eggs and beat on low speed until well combined.
3. Transfer the mixture into a 6-inch greased springform pan evenly.
4. With a piece of foil, cover the pan.
5. In the pot of Ninja Foodi, place 2 cups of water.
6. Arrange a "Reversible Rack" in the pot of Ninja Foodi.
7. Place the springform pan over the "Reversible Rack".
8. Close the Ninja Foodi with pressure lid and place the pressure valve to "Seal" position.
9. Select "Pressure" and set to "High" for 30 minutes.
10. Press "Start/Stop" to begin cooking.
11. Switch the valve to "Vent" and do a "Natural" release.
12. Place the pan onto a wire rack to cool slightly.
13. Meanwhile, in a small bowl, add the sour cream and remaining Truvia and beat until well combined.
14. Spread the cream mixture on the warm cake evenly.
15. Refrigerate for about 6-8 hours before serving.

Nutrition:

Calories: 182, Fats: 16.6g, Net Carbs: 2.1g, Carbs: 2.1g, Fiber: 0g, Sugar: 0.3g, Proteins: 6.4g, Sodium: 152mg

Mocha Cake

Prep Time: 15 minutes
Cooking time: 3 hours 37 minutes
Servings: 6

Ingredients:

- 2 ounces 70% dark chocolate, chopped finely
- ¾ cup butter, chopped
- ½ cup heavy cream
- 2 tablespoons instant coffee crystals
- 1 teaspoon organic vanilla extract
- 1/3 cup almond flour
- ¼ cup unsweetened cacao powder
- 1/8 teaspoon salt
- 5 large organic eggs
- 2/3 cup Erythritol

Directions:

1. Grease the pot of Ninja Foodi.
2. In a microwave-safe bowl, add the chocolate and butter and microwave on High for about 2 minutes or until melted completely, stirring after every 30 seconds.
3. Remove from the microwave and stir well.
4. Set aside to cool.
5. In a small bowl, add the heavy cream, coffee crystals, and vanilla extract and beat until well combined.
6. In another bowl, mix together the flour, cacao powder and salt.
7. In a large bowl, add the eggs and with an electric mixer, beat on high speed until slightly thickened.
8. Slowly, add the Erythritol and beat on high speed until thick and pale yellow.
9. Add the chocolate mixture and beat on low speed until well combined.
10. Add the flour mixture and mix until just combined.
11. Slowly, add the cream mixture and beat on medium speed until well combined.
12. In the prepared pot of Ninja Foodi, place the mixture.
13. Close the Ninja Foodi with crisping lid and select "Slow Cooker".
14. Set on "Low" for 2½-3½ hours.
15. Press "Start/Stop" to begin cooking.
16. Transfer the pan onto a wire rack to cool for about 10 minutes.
17. Carefully invert the cake onto the wire rack to cool completely.
18. Cut into desired-sized slices and serve.

Nutrition:

Calories: 407, Fats: 39.7g, Net Carbs: 3.3g, Carbs: 6.2g, Fiber: 2.9g, Sugar: 0.7g, Proteins: 9g, Sodium: 279mg

Printed in Great Britain
by Amazon